JAMES McNAIR's
GRILL
COOKBOOK

Photography by Patricia Brabant

Chronicle Books • San Francisco

Printed in Japan

Library of Congress
Cataloging-in-Publication Data
McNair, James K.
[Grill cookbook]
James McNair's Grill Cookbook
/James McNair;
Photography by Patricia Brabant.
p. cm.
Includes index.
ISBN 0-87701-719-0
ISBN 0-87701-710-7 (pbk.)
1. Barbecue cookery. 2. Broiling.
I. Brabant, Patricia.
II. Title. III. Title: Grill cookbook.
TX840.B3M44   1990
641.5'784—dc20   89-70848
                          CIP

Distributed in Canada by
Raincoast Books
112 East Third Avenue
Vancouver, British Columbia V5T 1C8

10 9 8 7 6 5 4

Chronicle Books
275 Fifth Street
San Francisco, California 94103

For John Richardson, my brother-in-law, who is also a good friend, a terrific dad to the world's greatest nephew, and one of the finest grill cooks I know.

Produced by The Rockpile Press, San Francisco and Lake Tahoe

Art direction, prop and food styling, and book design by James McNair

Editorial production assistance by Lin Cotton

Editorial and styling assistance by Ellen Quan

Photographic assistance by M. J. Murphy

Typography and mechanical production by Cleve Gallat and Charles N. Sublett of CTA Graphics

CONTENTS

A NEW CUISINE   5

SHELLFISH & FISH   13

POULTRY & MEATS   33

GRAINS, VEGETABLES, & FRUITS   65

MARINADES, GLAZES, & SAUCES   81

INDEX   94

ACKNOWLEDGMENTS   96

A NEW CUISINE

In recent years grilled fare has taken its rightful place as a distinct cuisine. It seems a bit ironic, however, that this current rage for cooking food directly over a smoldering fire is merely a variation on the world's primal cooking method.

When automobile magnate Henry Ford and his sideline-business partner Charles Kingsford marketed the first charcoal briquettes in 1923, cooking over fire was made easier. Imposing brick or stone barbecue pits dominated backyards in the early years. If you wanted something that could be moved around, you had to be inventive. During my childhood my father cooked scrumptious steaks and chicken on a covered grill he constructed from an unused oil barrel. With the introduction of the now-ubiquitous kettle grill by Weber-Stephen in the 1950s, the grilling craze was off and running. Unlike the Hula-Hoop of the same era, the grill has remained popular, never falling from fashion, and in recent years enthusiasm for grilled fare has escalated to fever pitch.

As with much of the rest of the American cooking scene, grilling has zoomed upscale. Grill cooks are no longer content with turning out simple hamburgers, although perfect renditions of that all-American treat remain impossible to beat. Today we're grilling rabbit and quail as well as chicken, an international array of sausages along with hot dogs, tofu and vegetables next to steaks, and fresh fruits instead of marshmallows.

Much of the current grilling mania stems from the countless trendy restaurants stretching from coast to coast that have adopted the cooking method first popularized in California. With all the interest, it is a wonder that any mesquite trees are left standing in the deserts of the Southwest and Mexico.

COMING TO TERMS

For decades most of us called all outdoor cooking over a fire barbecuing. Suddenly the word *grilling* popped up in contemporary recipes and trendy restaurants everywhere. Although most of us use the terms interchangeably, there are certain similarities and distinct differences. Put simply, barbecuing is always grilling, but grilling is not always barbecuing.

Grilling takes place on a metal grid rack set directly over a heat source, which may be smoldering coals, electric coils, or gas burners lined with lava stones. Foods cooked over wood or charcoal may be called barbecued, but most grilling is not barbecuing.

The time-honored and still-delicious practice of cooking meat on a backyard grill and basting it heavily with traditional tomato-based sauce is not actually barbecuing. To be truly authentic, as perfected in different ways in the Deep South and the Southwest, barbecuing occurs only in an enclosed unit over smoldering hardwood, an all-American technique worthy of its own book. Barbecued meat is cooked very slowly to create the characteristic smoky flavor and tender meat that literally falls from the bone.

BASTING BRUSHES. Stock several natural-bristle paintbrushes about two to three inches wide for oiling the grill rack and foods before cooking and for brushing foods with marinades or glazes during grilling. Long-handled brushes keep the cook a safe distance from the heat.

CLEANING BRUSH. Use a long-handled, stiff wire brush for cleaning grill racks. Look for brushes with steel scrapers attached to the back side for removing heavily burned-on food bits.

DRIP PANS. Keep disposable shallow heavy-duty foil pans on hand for catching drips when recipes specify grilling over indirect heat.

FIRE STARTER. For charcoal briquette fires, I recommend either a long-handled electric coil starter or a grill chimney, a straight-sided metal container with a heat-blocking wooden handle. See page 8 for an explanation of how each starter works.

HINGED WIRE GRILLS OR BASKETS. Foods that may prove troublesome to turn can be placed inside two wire grills that are hinged together on one side and have long handles on the other side. Seek out a variety of shapes and sizes, including ovals for holding whole fish and rectangles for fish fillets, shrimp, sliced vegetables, and other small pieces of foods. Mesh wire screens

Grill Equipment

Grills can be grouped into three categories based on the fuel used: charcoal, gas, and electric. Each type of grill embraces a wide array of models, ranging from inexpensive scaled-down portables to serious pieces of furniture with price tags to match.

CHARCOAL. This is definitely the method for those who grill only a few times a year or for people who enjoy the flavor and experience of cooking over charred wood. Charcoal-burning grills are less expensive than their gas or electric counterparts. Portable fireplace units, such as an iron grill stand imported from the Tuscany region of Italy, make year-round charcoal cookery possible even in frigid areas.

On the negative side, charcoal grills take longer to preheat than gas or electric grills and they are messy to clean up. Charcoal is also a more expensive fuel than either of the other two.

GAS. Surprisingly, nearly half of all the grills in use today are gas fueled. This is the direction for anyone who thinks building charcoal fires involves too much effort or who hasn't the time to wait for a charcoal fire to get hot. Gas grills are ready for cooking in only five to seven minutes and there is sufficient fuel for a long cooking period, unlike charcoal grilling, which requires the starting of replacement coals. Gas is a fairly inexpensive fuel and an easy-to-replace tank lasts through numerous cookings. Some avid grillers even install underground gas lines hooked directly to the grill. Plus, regulating the cooking temperature on gas-fueled grills is easier than with any other type.

Since most units have at least two burners, it is possible to maintain two temperatures at the same time. This allows for grilling fish over high heat while grilling vegetables over a lower flame, for example. Cleanup is a breeze since there are no messy ashes to discard and the heating elements burn away any cooking residues dripped onto the lava-rock lining. Some models come with removable grease trays that collect dripping fats and thus prevent flare-ups. Many newly designed kitchens include built-in gas grills, which permit almost-instant grilling any day of the year.

On the down side, gas units come with the most expensive price tags. Many grill cooks also still argue that the unique flavor imparted from cooking over charcoal is missing. Gas- or electric-grill devotees, however, emphatically state that true grill-cooking flavor comes from the marinades and from the drippings that burn on the lava stones in the same way as they do on charcoal, creating an aromatic smoke that surrounds the food. For those who still insist on authentic charcoal flavor but want the convenience of gas, there's the recent introduction of ten-hour-burning charcoal briquettes for use in some gas grills. It is also possible to get good smoky flavor by adding presoaked wood chips directly on the heated lava stones or in a perforated metal container placed under the grill rack.

ELECTRIC. Grills powered by electricity heat up even faster than gas models and have the advantage of easily controlled temperature. They are also usually the lightest to move around.

Negatively speaking, electrical coils don't get as hot as charcoal or gas fires. These grills must be used near a power source and may require new electrical lines to reach the cookout area.

OPEN VERSUS CLOSED

Grill cooks can't agree on whether covered grills or open units are best. Ideally, we'd own one of each type for various uses—an open grill for preparing foods that cook quickly, such as thin cuts of meat, steaks, chops, or fillets, and a covered unit for foods that require longer cooking, such as roasts, whole fish, or turkeys. Since budget or space restraints prevent that option for many, a covered grill with a movable rack or fuel grate to allow variation when cooking without the cover may be the best option.

Although many cooks see the immovable grid and fuel grate of the popular Weber kettle as a disadvantage because distance from the heat source cannot be regulated, the manufacturer and loyal kettle grillers defend the product and emphasize that the reflected heat from the domed cover reduces cooking time and keeps foods moist. Covered grills also virtually eliminate flare-ups, which can burn the exterior of foods.

Every recipe in this book that calls for an open grill can be adapted to covered cooking. Check your grill manufacturer's manual for approximate cooking times; test the food for doneness earlier than the given times to be sure it is cooked the way you like it.

made for grills or heavy-duty wire pizza screens from restaurant supply houses also keep small pieces of food from falling through the grill.

MITTS. To avoid burns, choose heavy-duty kitchen mitts with long cuffs.

SKEWERS. Speared small food pieces are easily managed. Bamboo skewers leave only tiny holes in food, but must be soaked in water about 20 minutes before using to prevent ends from incinerating. Metal skewers are always ready to use, but get very hot during cooking; turn with tongs or mitts. To prevent foods from twisting on metal skewers, choose the flat-sided type.

SPATULA. A stainless-steel spatula with a long, wide blade and an angled neck attached to a wooden handle works best for turning or removing fish or other delicate foods. Check restaurant-supply houses if not available in kitchenware shops.

THERMOMETER. An instant-read meat thermometer can be probed into foods that are at least one inch thick for quick, accurate readings of internal temperature.

TONGS. Choose long-handled spring-loaded tongs made of stainless steel. Buy two pair, one for moving coals and another for easy turning of foods. Do not use forks, as they pierce foods and allow juices to escape.

The Grill Fire

FUEL FOR FIRE

GAS. Liquid propane tanks, obtained from grill dealers or hardware stores, are easily replaced as needed.

CHARCOAL BRIQUETTES. Composed of sawdust, coal, wood chips, and such fillers as sand, and bound with a petroleum-based substance, this is the most commonly burned charcoal in the United States, where an estimated 25 billion briquettes go up in backyard smoke each year. Those sold as match-light briquettes have been impregnated with chemical lighter fluid.

LUMP CHARCOAL. Chunks of natural pure-carbon residue from the controlled burning of hardwood such as alder, hickory, or mesquite starts quicker, burns about twice as hot, and smells cleaner than charcoal briquettes. It throws more sparks, however, and is not nearly as easy to locate, although the demand from the grill-restaurant craze has made lump charcoal, especially mesquite, more readily available. Generally, you'll need only half as much lump charcoal as briquettes for a fire of similar heat intensity.

Preparing a fire in an electric or gas grill is as easy as throwing a switch or turning on a jet and striking a match. An electric grill is ready for cooking in about three to four minutes; a gas fire is preheated in only a couple of minutes longer. With each unit, follow directions in the manufacturer's manual for preheating for direct-heat or indirect grilling.

To start a fire with lump charcoal or match-light briquettes, simply mound the coals on top of crumpled newspaper and ignite the paper with a match. Lump coals should be ready for cooking in about 10 minutes, and match-light briquettes in about 15 minutes.

To start a fire with a metal chimney, add crumpled newspaper to the bottom section of this inexpensive, straight-sided metal container. Set the chimney on the fire grate, pour charcoal into the top section, and light the newspaper with a match. After about 30 minutes, the underside of the top coals should be white-hot and ready to use. Holding the chimney by its wooden handle, turn the coals out onto the grate. The chimney is also an easy way to keep extra coals ready for adding when a long-burning fire is required. After turning out the coals, start a second batch of coals in the chimney set over a hibachi, in a large terra-cotta plant saucer, or on a heavy-gauge metal sheet. They'll be ready to add when the original fire begins to burn too low.

To start a fire with an electric starter, position the long-handled device so that the coil is directly on the fuel grate. Mound the coals on top of the coil and plug the starter into a nearby outlet or heavy-duty extension cord. Remove the coil after about 10 minutes and carefully transfer it to a fire-retardant surface well out of reach of children or pets. The fire should be ready in about 20 minutes.

To start a fire with charcoal lighter fluid, saturate a pile of briquettes with the fluid, then ignite with a long-handled match. Although purists object to the use of lighter fluid, numerous tests demonstrate that after the fire is ready for cooking, in 25 to 30 minutes, the fluid is completely burned away and no chemical or off-flavor is imparted to the food.

To start a fire with starter logs or blocks, crumble a log over a charcoal mound or add one or two small blocks to the mound. Ignite with a match. The fire should be ready in 15 to 20 minutes.

DIRECT-HEAT OR INDIRECT GRILLING

With direct-heat grilling, food cooks right over the heat source. Indirect grilling offsets the food from the fire, a practice highly recommended for good-sized cuts of meat, large whole fish or turkeys, or foods with dripping marinades or fat.

To prepare a charcoal fire for direct-heat grilling, allow the mound of coals to burn undisturbed until lightly covered with white ash and glowing but no longer flaming. Using long-handled tongs, distribute the coals in an even layer over the fuel grate. If you wish to create areas with varying degrees of heat in order to move food around and help prevent flare-ups, leave a few coals banked together and spread the others out evenly, allotting a little space with no coals.

To prepare a charcoal fire for indirect grilling in a covered grill, allow the coals to reach the glowing ash stage, then position them along two sides on the fuel grate. In most cases you'll want to add a heavy-duty foil pan in between to catch any drips from the food, marinade, or glaze that can cause flare-ups that may incinerate the food's exterior during prolonged cooking.

FLAVORFUL SMOKE

Since charcoal makes a much more satisfactory grill fuel than wood chunks, it is best to use wood only for imparting smoky flavor. Today it seems that mesquite madness has given way to chips or cuttings from every imaginable wood packaged for the grill—alder, apple, cherry, grapevines, hickory, maple, oak, peach, pecan. As a general rule, the stronger-flavored woods—hickory, mesquite, and oak—impart the most taste to grilled fare. The added flavor from fruit tree or grapevine cuttings is so indistinguishable that they seem a waste of time and money.

To secure the best smoky fragrance from wood chips, soak them in water for about 30 minutes before adding to the fire. To use wood chips in a gas or electric grill, indoors or out, punch several small holes in a heavy-duty foil container, fill with moistened chips, and position on the grate underneath the grill rack.

Recipes in numerous other sources suggest adding flavor by throwing fresh herb cuttings onto the fire or by using herb sprigs to brush oils or marinades on the grilling foods. My own experiments conclude that herbs are best used directly on the foods instead of wasted in the fire or employed as brushes where they add no distinguishable flavor.

Grilling

SAFE GRILLING

Do not grill indoors unless a unit is specifically designed for use in a fireplace or is built into the kitchen.

Avoid charcoal fires in high winds.

Never squirt charcoal lighter fluid directly onto a fire.

Position a charcoal grill over a nonflammable surface in case embers fall through the air vents. If you must grill over a wooden deck, generously wet the area before starting a fire or position the grill over a large metal pan, such as an automotive oil-spill tray.

When handling grill parts during cooking, wear heavy-duty mitts to avoid burns.

Avoid wearing garments with flowing sleeves during grilling.

Use long-handled cooking tools.

Carefully lift the grill cover away from you to avoid being burned by steam and smoke.

Never attempt to move a hot grill.

To determine when a grill is ready for cooking, wait until the fire is no longer flaming, then remove the grill rack and hold your hand at the rack level. If recipes call for a "hot" fire, the coals should still be glowing a bit red but no longer flaming and you should be able to keep your hand at rack level for three to four seconds. A "moderate" fire is when the coals are lightly coated with gray ash, no longer red, and you can hold your hand at rack level for five to six seconds. To help prevent flames that can overcook food surfaces, be certain that the fire is not too hot before adding the food.

Start with a clean grill rack that is absolutely free of any burned-on food from previous use. The ideal time to clean the rack is immediately after each use, but all grill cooks forget the cleanup detail from time to time. A stiff wire brush (see sidebar, page 6) easily does the trick.

Position the grill rack in place and preheat it for several minutes; a properly heated rack adds nice brown grid marks to the surface of the food in about two minutes. Just before placing the food on the grill, brush the rack with vegetable oil to prevent food from sticking.

Shrimp, scallops, whole fish or fillets, sliced vegetables, and other foods that are difficult to turn with tongs, or could burn quickly in the time it takes to turn them individually, can be skewered or placed in a hinged grill basket (see sidebar, page 6) for easy manipulation. When using bamboo skewers, soak them well before threading to prevent the ends from burning. To keep foods from rolling around on bamboo or round metal skewers, thread them on two parallel skewers positioned about ½-inch apart.

In general, it is best to thread only one type of food per skewer so that each skewer can be taken off the grill as soon as the food is done. For example, thread meat cubes together, impale fast-cooking tomatoes on another skewer, and skewer slower-cooking carrots by themselves. Slip the various foods off the skewers and combine them on the serving plate.

To avoid flare-ups that can heavily char the surface of the food before the inside is done, control the fire temperature of a charcoal grill with a cover and air vents; adjust the dials to control gas or electrical heat. Fatty foods or those with flame-enhancing sugary marinades or glazes are best cooked with indirect heat, usually over a pan for catching fuel-flaming drips. In any case, avoid squirting coals with water, which causes unappetizing flying ashes to settle on food.

Turn foods as directed in grill recipes. Some require frequent turning and brushing with marinades or glazes; others may need to be turned only once, about halfway through cooking. Use tongs or a large metal spatula to turn foods; forks puncture the surface and allow flavorful juices to drain away.

Suggested cooking times are always approximate. The actual cooking time depends on the particular grill, the temperature of the fire, and the preference of the cook. I always begin testing a bit earlier than I think food may be ready, since even a few seconds over a direct fire can make a tremendous difference. Follow the suggested test for doneness in each recipe.

As soon as food is done to your liking, carefully transfer it to a heat-resistant platter or tray and follow recipe directions for cutting and serving. Some meats need a few minutes to rest before slicing. Using a stiff wire brush, quickly scrub the grill rack free of all burned-on debris.

If there are still fairly good-sized pieces of charcoal smoldering after the food is cooked, cover the grill and close all air vents to cut off the oxygen supply and smother the fire. To rekindle in the future, start with some new coals and add the partially burned ones on top.

The recipes that follow were chosen to illustrate the wide variety of foods that can be grilled successfully. At the end of the book, you will discover a collection of marinades, glazes, and sauces that can be matched up with the grill recipes or used to create your own grilled fare.

Avoid dumping ashes where they might start a fire or where pets or people might come in direct contact with them. Dispose of cold ashes in a covered metal can.

GRILLING AND HEALTH

Grilling reduces fat intake since much of the fat drips away from the food instead of being reabsorbed during cooking.

Some cause for alarm was raised in recent years when the toxins that result from burning fat during grilling were identified as the same culprits found in industrial pollution and cigarette smoke. Good news comes from more recent studies, however. They report that a person would have to consume tons of grilled food every day for many years in order for these potential carcinogens to prove harmful.

SHELLFISH & FISH

Grilling is one of the best methods for cooking the waters' harvests. It is easy and quick and imparts special flavor without masking freshness or the unique taste of fish, shellfish, or bivalves.

Most fish should be grilled about four inches directly above a hot fire in an open grill. Large whole fish that require longer cooking are more successfully prepared in a covered grill over indirect heat.

Since fish is fragile, a hinged wire basket or wire mesh screen laid over the grill rack helps in turning fish and is almost essential when grilling small whole fish, fillets, or such small shellfish as scallops.

Although countless recipes from other sources call for grilling fish until the flesh flakes, in my opinion it is overcooked by that point. Cook until the flesh has just turned from translucent to opaque. Generally, fish takes about 10 minutes total cooking time per inch; measure at the thickest portion. To test for opaqueness, insert a small, sharp knife into the thickest part of the fish and gently pry the meat apart so you can see the flesh. Another method is to insert a slender bamboo skewer into the fish at the thickest part; the fish is ready if the skewer meets very little resistance as it enters.

Tests for shellfish doneness are included with each recipe.

GRILLED FISH RECIPES IN OTHER JAMES McNAIR BOOKS

BAR & GRILL COOKBOOK:

Grilled Ahi Tuna with Oregano Salsa Verde, page 73

Grilled Shrimp and Scallop Salad, page 20

Grilled Swordfish with Mexican Grapefruit Salad, page 17

JAMES McNAIR'S SALMON COOKBOOK:

Grilled Salmon, page 42

Grilled Fennel-Stuffed Baby Salmon, page 44

Barbecued Salmon, page 47

Corn-Wrapped Salmon and Scallops, page 49

Teriyaki, page 50

Herb-Marinated Shrimp

Herbed Olive Oil Marinade (page 82)
2 pounds medium-sized to large
    shrimp or prawns in the shell
Vegetable oil for brushing grill rack
    or wire basket

My brother-in-law John Richardson sets out mounds of these delectables as an appetizer. The communal shelling is a guaranteed icebreaker; but the shrimp may also be arranged on individual plates. For a fancier presentation or for fastidious guests, peel the shrimp before serving them. To prepare as a hearty salad, toss peeled grilled shrimp with cooked pasta, minced green onion and fresh herbs, and a lemony vinaigrette.

No sauce is necessary, but you may offer melted butter, Creole Mustard Cream (page 88), or Spicy Sweet-and-Sour Sauce (page 91) for dipping.

Prepare the marinade in a large, shallow nonreactive container. Add the shrimp or prawns and turn to coat evenly. Cover and let stand at room temperature for 30 minutes or refrigerate for up to 3 hours.

Prepare an open grill for hot direct-heat cooking as described on pages 8–10 or according to the manufacturer's instructions.

When the fire is ready, remove the shrimp or prawns and reserve the marinade. If the shellfish are large, lightly brush the grill rack with vegetable oil and place the shrimp directly on the rack. Arrange smaller shrimp in an oiled hinged grill basket or on a piece of wire mesh. Cook, turning once and brushing frequently with the reserved marinade, until the shrimp shells turn bright pink and the meat is just opaque, about 6 to 8 minutes total cooking time.

Serve hot or at room temperature.

Serves 8 as a starter, or 4 as a main course.

Oysters with Champagne Cream

Clams or mussels may be cooked in the same way. Serve on a bed of heated rock salt, if desired. Alternatively, oysters can be shucked and skewered before grilling.

Prepare the sauce; reserve.

Choose oysters that are tightly closed or close when handled. Using a stiff brush, scrub the shells under running cold water. Transfer to a plastic bag or covered container and refrigerate until a few minutes before cooking.

Prepare an open grill for hot direct-heat cooking as described on pages 8–10 or according to the manufacturer's instructions.

When the fire is ready, place the oysters, flat side up, on the grill rack and cook until the shells just open, about 3 minutes; discard any that fail to open. Transfer the oysters to a work area, being careful not to spill the tasty juices. Holding each oyster in a mitt-gloved hand, use an oyster knife to pull off and discard the top shell. Should the oyster cling to the top shell, gently scrape it into the bottom shell. Spoon some of the reserved sauce over each oyster and return the shell to the grill. Cook until the sauce is bubbly and begins to brown around the edges.

Top each oyster with chervil or parsley and add a dollop of caviar, if using. Serve immediately.

Serves 6 as a starter, or 3 as a main course.

VARIATION: For a simpler dish, omit the sauce and garnishes; top the grilled oysters with a dollop of your favorite fresh salsa.

Champagne Cream (page 87)
3 dozen medium-sized oysters in the shell
Fresh chervil or parsley leaflets
Caviar for garnish (optional)

Scallops with Squid-Ink Pasta

¼ cup (½ stick) unsalted butter
1 tablespoon minced or pressed garlic
Salt
Freshly ground black pepper
½ pound squid-ink pasta or other
    favorite pasta
24 large sea scallops
    (about 18 ounces)
Fruity olive oil, preferably
    extra-virgin, for brushing
    scallops
Vegetable oil for brushing grill rack
Red and gold sweet pepper strips or
    cutouts for garnish

A halo of grilled sweet-tasting scallops surrounding black pasta is a showstopping first course or light entrée. Look for fresh or dried pasta flavored and colored with squid ink in takeout pasta shops or specialty food markets. Or make your own from a reliable recipe. The scallops are also good served on their own or with almost any favorite pasta or rice.

Prepare an open grill for hot direct-heat cooking as described on pages 8–10 or according to the manufacturer's instructions.

Melt the butter in a small saucepan over low heat. Add the garlic and simmer about 5 minutes. Strain and discard garlic. Season butter with salt and pepper to taste and keep warm.

Fill a large pot with water and place it over high heat. While the water comes to a boil, quickly rinse the scallops under cold running water and pat dry with paper toweling. Brush all over with olive oil and season to taste with salt and pepper. Add the pasta to the boiling water, stir well, and cook until *al dente*, about 1 minute for fresh or up to 15 minutes for dried. Drain and transfer to a heated bowl. Toss with the garlic butter and keep warm.

When the fire is ready, lightly brush the grill rack with vegetable oil. Place the scallops on the rack and grill 1 minute. Turn and grill second side until scallops are just opaque, about 1 minute.

Arrange the pasta in the middle of 4 warmed plates and place the grilled scallops around the perimeter. Garnish with sweet pepper and serve immediately.

Serves 4 as a first course or light main course.

Lobster with Lemon-Chive Butter

1 cup Composed Butter (page 86),
    prepared with chives and lemon
4 live North Atlantic lobsters
    (about 1½ to 2 pounds *each*)
Vegetable oil for brushing grill rack
2 lemons, cut in half horizontally
    and all pulp removed with a
    small knife and spoon (optional)

SUGGESTED ACCOMPANIMENT
Grilled corn on the cob

To dress up this dish, remove the cooked lobster meat from the tail, slice the meat ¼ inch thick, and reassemble the meat in the shell. Carefully remove the meat from the claws and arrange meat alongside tail. If you choose to leave the lobsters in their shells, be sure to provide nutcrackers for breaking into the claws. Spiny or rock lobster tails or cracked crab can also be grilled this way.

Prepare the butter; reserve.

Bring a large pot of water to a boil. Plunge the lobsters head first into the boiling water and cook for about 2 minutes to kill them. Remove to a tray to drain.

Prepare an open grill for hot direct-heat cooking as described on pages 8–10 or according to the manufacturer's instructions.

When the fire is ready, lightly brush the grill rack with vegetable oil. Place the lobster, top side down, on the grill and cook for 4 minutes. Turn the lobster and cook until the meat is opaque when the tail is cut into with a small sharp knife, about 4 to 5 minutes longer. Remove the lobster to a work surface, twist off the claws, and return them to the grill for about 3 minutes longer.

Meanwhile, melt the reserved butter and distribute among the lemon shells or 4 individual dipping bowls. Serve alongside the hot lobsters.

Serves 4.

Fish Steaks with Gingered Mango Sauce

Gingered Mango Sauce (page 92)
Four ¾-inch-thick tuna or swordfish
    steaks (about 7 ounces *each*)
Vegetable oil for brushing grill rack
Peanut or other high-quality
    vegetable oil for brushing fish
Salt
Freshly ground black pepper
Lime slices for garnish
Fresh mint or marjoram sprigs
    for garnish

SUGGESTED ACCOMPANIMENT
Grilled seasonal vegetables

Steaks from large, whole firm-fleshed fish may be cut crosswise from the center of the fish or on the diagonal from one of the fillets. Tuna is most often the fish of choice for grilling on the West Coast; East Coast residents are more likely to opt for swordfish. Bluefish, mahi-mahi, salmon, sea bass, shark, or sturgeon are other good candidates.

Alternative sauces include Citrus Salsa (page 90), Pineapple Salsa (page 90), or Composed Butters (page 86).

Prepare the sauce; keep warm.

Prepare an open grill for hot direct-heat cooking as described on pages 8–10 or according to the manufacturer's instructions.

Quickly rinse the fish under cold running water and pat dry with paper toweling.

When the fire is ready, lightly brush the grill rack with vegetable oil. Brush the fish with peanut or other vegetable oil and sprinkle with salt and pepper to taste. Place fish on the grill rack directly over heat for about 1 minute. Reposition the steaks on the same side at a 45-degree angle to original position to create classic crosshatched grill marks. Cook, turning once, until the flesh is just opaque when tested by cutting with a small, sharp knife, about 6 to 8 minutes total cooking time.

Spoon the reserved sauce onto 4 plates. Top with the steaks and garnish with lime slices and herb sprigs. Serve hot.

Serves 4.

Spicy Catfish Fillets with Remoulade Sauce

Try this technique with small fillets cut from other fish, such as snapper or trout.

Prepare the sauce; cover and refrigerate until a few minutes before serving.

In a small bowl, combine the peppers, thyme, garlic, and salt; mix well.

Quickly rinse the fish under cold running water and pat dry with paper toweling. Spread fillets out on a tray and pat each side with the seasoning mixture, pressing the spices into the flesh with your fingertips. Let stand for about 30 minutes at room temperature, or cover and refrigerate for up to 3 hours; remove from refrigerator about 20 minutes before cooking.

Prepare an open grill for hot direct-heat cooking as described on pages 8–10 or according to the manufacturer's instructions.

When the fire is ready, lightly brush the grill rack or the inside of a hinged wire basket with vegetable oil. Lightly brush the fish with peanut or other vegetable oil. Place fish on the grill rack or in the hinged wire basket directly over heat. Cook, turning once, until the thickest portion of flesh is just opaque when tested by cutting with a small, sharp knife, about 5 to 6 minutes total cooking time. Serve immediately with the reserved sauce and grilled vegetables.

Serves 6.

Remoulade Sauce (page 89)
2 teaspoons ground cayenne pepper
2 teaspoons freshly ground
    black pepper
1 teaspoon freshly ground
    white pepper
2 tablespoons minced fresh thyme,
    or 2 teaspoons finely crumbled
    dried thyme
1 tablespoon minced or pressed garlic
1 teaspoon salt
1½ pounds catfish fillets,
    about ½ inch thick
Vegetable oil for brushing grill rack
    or wire basket
Peanut or other high-quality
    vegetable oil for brushing fish

SUGGESTED ACCOMPANIMENT
Grilled summer squash

Whole Fish with Grilled Vegetable Salsa

1 whole firm-fleshed fish
    (5 to 7 pounds), cleaned
Olive oil for brushing fish
Salt
Freshly ground black pepper
Vegetable oil for brushing
    wire basket
Grilled Vegetable Salsa (page 90)
Fresh herb sprigs for garnish

Red snapper, rockfish, redfish, or other firm-fleshed fish are marvelous choices for grilling whole. The head and tail may be removed before cooking if you have squeamish diners.

As an accompaniment, grill some potatoes alongside the fish and toss them in sour cream and minced chives or dill or in a vinaigrette for a tasty twist on traditional potato salad.

Prepare a covered grill for hot indirect-heat cooking as described on pages 8–10 or according to the manufacturer's instructions. Place a drip pan in the center of the fire grate.

When the fire is ready, quickly rinse the fish inside and out under cold running water and pat dry with paper toweling. Brush the fish all over with olive oil and season to taste with salt and pepper. Brush the inside of a hinged wire basket with vegetable oil and place the fish inside. Transfer to grill over drip pan. Cover and cook, turning once and brushing occasionally with olive oil, until the flesh is just opaque when tested by cutting into the thickest part with a small, sharp knife, about 35 to 45 minutes total cooking time. If necessary to maintain temperature, adjust dampers and add additional coals to the fire after about 25 minutes.

Prepare the vegetables for the salsa. Place them on the grill rack around the fish, then finish salsa as directed.

Transfer the fish to a heated platter, surround it with the warm salsa, and garnish with herbs. To serve, use a wide spatula to cut down to the bone and lift off sections.

Serves 4 to 6.

Trout with Toasted Pecan Butter

Toasted Pecan Butter (page 87)
Champagne Cream (page 87)
6 trout (about ½ pound *each*), cleaned
    and preferably boned
Peanut or other high-quality
    vegetable oil for brushing fish
Salt
Freshly ground black pepper
Vegetable oil for brushing grill rack
    or wire basket

SUGGESTED ACCOMPANIMENTS
Wild rice
Grilled beets

This recipe was inspired by a similar preparation I've enjoyed at one of my all-time favorite dining spots: Commander's Palace in New Orleans. There the trout is panfried and the pecans are covered with a meunière sauce. Although the grilled fish is quite tasty with only the pecans, a crown of Champagne Cream makes an even more luxurious dish.

Prepare the pecan butter, reserving about half of the pecans for garnish. Prepare the Champagne Cream. Set toppings aside.

Prepare an open grill for hot direct-heat cooking as described on pages 8–10 or according to the manufacturer's instructions.

When the fire is ready, quickly rinse the trout inside and out under cold running water and pat dry with paper toweling. Lightly brush the trout with peanut oil and sprinkle with salt and pepper to taste. Lightly brush the grill rack or inside of a hinged wire basket with vegetable oil. Place fish on the grill rack or in the hinged wire basket directly over heat. Cook, turning once, until the flesh is just opaque when tested by cutting into the thickest part with a small, sharp knife, 6 to 8 minutes total cooking time.

Using a wide metal spatula, transfer the trout to preheated plates. Top each with a dollop of pecan butter, sprinkle with reserved toasted pecans, and spoon reserved Champagne Cream over the top. Serve immediately.

Serves 6.

Skewered Fish

Herbed Olive Oil Marinade (page 82)
1½ pounds firm-fleshed fish fillets
White Butter (optional; page 86)
1 large lemon, thinly sliced, seeded,
      and slices cut in half
1 large red or gold sweet pepper,
      seeds and membranes discarded,
      cut into 1-inch squares
Vegetable oil for brushing grill rack

SUGGESTED ACCOMPANIMENT
Herbed rice

Choose a firm-fleshed fish such as sea bass, shark, or monkfish for this dish.

Using a combination of parsley and thyme, prepare the marinade; reserve.

Quickly rinse the fish under cold running water and pat dry with paper toweling. Cut the fish into 1-inch cubes and add to the marinade, turning to coat well. Cover and let stand for 30 minutes at room temperature, or refrigerate up to 3 hours; remove from the refrigerator about 20 minutes before cooking.

Prepare the butter sauce, if using; reserve.

Prepare an open grill for hot direct-heat cooking as described on pages 8–10 or according to the manufacturer's instructions. If using bamboo skewers, soak in water for about 20 minutes before threading fish on them.

Remove the fish and reserve the marinade. Thread the fish on metal or presoaked bamboo skewers alternately with the lemon slices and sweet pepper pieces. Brush the lemon and pepper with the reserved marinade.

When the fire is ready, brush the grill rack with vegetable oil. Place the skewers on the rack, and grill, turning several times and basting frequently with the marinade, until the fish is just opaque when tested by cutting with a small, sharp knife, about 8 to 10 minutes total cooking time.

Serve immediately with the butter sauce, if desired.

Serves 4.

POULTRY & MEATS

Small young whole, split, or disjointed chickens or other fowl are among the best fare to come off a grill. Skinned pieces grill quickly directly over an open fire. Poultry with the skin attached cooks best over indirect heat in a covered grill, which prevents flare-ups caused by the melting of the skin's fat into the fire.

To grill a turkey or large whole chicken, grill breast side down until well browned, then turn and cook, basting occasionally, until the juices run clear when pierced near the thigh joint, about 20 minutes per pound.

Only the most tender cuts of lamb, pork, veal, and beef should be subjected to the intense heat of a grill. In spite of instructions to the contrary in countless other grill recipe sources, chops, steaks, or burgers will retain more of their natural juices if turned several times during grilling. Since large pieces of meat continue to cook after taking them off the grill, remove a few minutes before you would consider the meat done, or when the internal temperature of the thickest portion of the meat registers about five to ten degrees less than the guideline indicated on a meat thermometer.

Always bring poultry and meats to room temperature before grilling.

GRILLED POULTRY & MEAT RECIPES IN OTHER JAMES McNAIR BOOKS

CHICKEN:

Grilled Drumsticks with Cumberland Marinade, page 78

Grilled Young Chickens with Raspberry Marinade, page 78

Grilled Chicken Breast Hoisin, page 80

Chicken Breast Yakitori, page 82

Chicken Sate with Peanut Sauce, page 82

Barbecued Chicken, page 84

Smoked Chicken Salad with Blueberry Dressing, page 86

Chicken Boudin Blanc, page 88

JAMES McNAIR'S BEEF COOKBOOK:

Cocktail Patty Melts, page 20

Sweet and Tangy Beef Salad, page 23

Corn-Stuffed Steak, page 24

Grilled Steak Fajitas, page 26

Grilled Steak with Peanut Sauce, page 29

Korean Barbecued Beef, page 31

Middle Eastern Kabobs, page 32

Garlic Steak Sandwich, page 35

Spicy Ground Beef Patties, page 37

Hamburgers, page 38

Spicy Young Chicken

Chili-Coconut Marinade (page 83)
Four 1-pound poussins, whole or
   split, or four 1½-pound Rock
   Cornish game hens, whole or
   split
Spicy Sweet-and-Sour Dipping Sauce
   (page 91)
Vegetable oil for brushing grill rack
Fresh cilantro (coriander) sprigs
   for garnish

SUGGESTED ACCOMPANIMENT
White rice, preferably basmati,
   cooked in unsweetened
   coconut milk

Contemporary American grilling has been greatly influenced by new Americans from Southeast Asia, as this recipe shows. Serving the dipping sauce in a hollowed-out pepper adds a whimsical touch.

Prepare the marinade; reserve.

Quickly rinse the poussins or Cornish hens under cold running water and pat dry with paper toweling. Place in a nonreactive shallow container, pour the marinade over, and turn to coat thoroughly. Cover and refrigerate for at least 8 hours or as long as 24 hours. Return to room temperature before cooking.

Prepare the dipping sauce; reserve.

Prepare a covered grill for moderate indirect cooking as described on pages 8–10 or according to the manufacturer's instructions.

When the fire is ready, lightly brush the grill rack with vegetable oil. Remove the birds and reserve the marinade. Place the birds on the grill rack, breast side down, and cook for 2 minutes to sear. Turn and cook on backs for 2 minutes to sear. Cover the grill and cook, turning every 8 to 10 minutes and brushing frequently with the marinade, until the juices run clear when the birds are pierced with a fork near the joint, about 25 to 30 minutes total cooking time.

Arrange birds on preheated plates with bowls of the dipping sauce alongside. Garnish with cilantro and serve immediately.

Serves 4.

Pineapple Chicken

For a stellar sandwich, serve a warm pineapple-infused chicken breast on a buttered, toasted sesame bun with Garlic Sauce (page 88) or Red Hot Chili Mayonnaise (page 89), a slice of grilled pineapple, and a few sprigs of fresh cilantro.

Prepare the marinade; reserve.

Discard the tendons and any connecting tissue or fat from the chicken breasts; separate the little fillet and use it for another purpose or leave it attached and tuck it under the larger muscle. Place breast pieces between 2 sheets of waxed paper and pound with a wooden mallet, the flat side of a cleaver, or other flat instrument to a uniform thickness of about ½ inch.

Place pounded breasts in a shallow nonreactive container and cover with the reserved marinade, rubbing it well into all sides of the chicken. Cover and marinate at room temperature for 2 hours, or in the refrigerator for at least 6 hours or as long as overnight. Return the chicken to room temperature before grilling.

Prepare an open grill for moderate direct-heat cooking as described on pages 8–10 or according to the manufacturer's instructions.

When the fire is ready, lightly brush the grill rack with vegetable oil. Remove the chicken and reserve the marinade. Place the chicken and the pineapple slices on the grill rack and cook, turning once and basting occasionally with the marinade, until the chicken is done but still moist inside and the pineapple slices are tender and lightly browned, about 8 to 12 minutes total cooking time.

Arrange chicken and pineapple on preheated plates and garnish with cilantro.

Serves 4.

Pineapple Teriyaki Marinade
    (page 84)
4 small to medium-sized boned and
    skinned chicken breast halves
Vegetable oil for brushing grill rack
4 fresh pineapple slices or wedges,
    peeled and cored
Fresh cilantro (coriander) sprigs
    for garnish

SUGGESTED ACCOMPANIMENT
Fried sweet potato chips or sticks

Chili-Marinated Turkey with Pineapple Salsa

Here, in a change of pace from the traditional roasted turkey, a fiery marinade is tempered by a tangy sweet salsa. A boned and skinned half turkey breast may be substituted for the tender fillets; double the cooking time.

Prepare the marinade; reserve.

Quickly rinse the turkey fillets under cold running water and pat dry with paper toweling. Place in a shallow nonreactive container, pour the marinade over, and turn to coat thoroughly. Cover and refrigerate for at least 8 hours or as long as 24 hours. Return to room temperature before cooking.

Prepare the salsa; reserve.

Prepare an open grill for moderate direct-heat cooking as described on pages 8–10 or according to the manufacturer's instructions.

When the fire is ready, lightly brush the grill rack with vegetable oil. Remove the turkey fillets and brush off excess marinade with your fingertips. Place the turkey on the grill rack for about 7 to 8 minutes, then turn and cook until done but still juicy inside, about 7 to 8 minutes longer. Remove to a cutting surface, cover loosely with foil, and let stand for about 5 minutes. Cut on a slight diagonal into slices about ¼ inch thick.

Serve turkey slices with the reserved salsa alongside. Garnish with the herb sprigs.

Serves 4 to 6.

Chili Marinade (page 84)
4 skinned turkey breast fillets
    (about ½ pound *each*)
Pineapple Salsa or
    Citrus Salsa (page 90)
Vegetable oil for brushing grill rack
Fresh epazote, cilantro, or
    mint sprigs for garnish

SUGGESTED ACCOMPANIMENT
Rice salad

Duck Breast with Red Wine Jelly

This is a simplified interpretation of a recipe from Rosie of the Calistoga Inn that was awarded first place when I was a judge for the North Lake Tahoe Autumn Food and Wine Jubilee. Although Rosie uses Cabernet Sauvignon for the jelly, I enjoy port in the marinade and jelly. To serve as a salad, toss mixed young salad greens, toasted walnuts, and apple slices in a vinaigrette made with the same wine used in the jelly. Arrange on plates and top with the duck slices.

Wine and Orange Marinade
(page 85)
Red Wine Jelly (page 85)
4 boned duck breasts,
trimmed of excess fat
Vegetable oil for brushing grill rack

Prepare the marinade and the jelly; reserve.

Quickly rinse the duck breasts under cold running water and pat dry with paper toweling. Prick the skin in several places with a sharp knife and place breasts in a shallow nonreactive container, pour the marinade over, and turn to coat thoroughly. Cover and refrigerate for at least 8 hours or as long as 24 hours. Return to room temperature before cooking.

Prepare a covered grill for moderate indirect-heat cooking as described on pages 8–10 or according to the manufacturer's instructions. Soak about 2 cups flavorful wood chips. Position a drip pan in the center of the fuel grate.

When the fire is ready, add the presoaked wood chips to the fire. Lightly brush the grill rack with vegetable oil. Remove the duck from the marinade and place on the rack directly over the coals, skin side down. Sear for about 2 minutes, then turn and sear second side for about 2 minutes. Reposition duck breasts over the drip pan, cover the grill, and cook, turning several times, until medium-rare when tested by cutting with a small, sharp knife, about 10 minutes total cooking time.

Transfer the duck to a cutting surface to cool for about 5 minutes. Meanwhile, heat about 1 cup of the wine jelly in a saucepan over low heat until melted. Slice the duck breasts at a slight angle into about 6 bite-sized pieces, keeping each sliced breast together in original shape, and brush all over with the warm jelly. Arrange on plates and serve immediately.

Serves 4.

Gorgonzola-Stuffed Quail

8 quail

GORGONZOLA STUFFING
1 cup crumbled creamy mild
    Gorgonzola or other blue cheese
½ cup minced fresh basil
2 tablespoons drained, minced
    sun-dried tomatoes in olive oil

Salt
Freshly ground black pepper
8 thin slices bacon or pancetta
    (Italian-style unsmoked bacon)
Vegetable oil for brushing grill rack
½ cup (1 stick) unsalted butter,
    melted
Large radicchio or lettuce leaves
    (optional)
Fresh basil sprigs for garnish

SUGGESTED ACCOMPANIMENT
Grilled endive

Fragrant smoke from presoaked wood chips imparts extra dimension to the flavor of these succulent little birds. Although boning takes time, it adds immeasurable dining pleasure.

Quickly rinse the quail under cold running water and pat dry with paper toweling. Place each bird breast side down and cut down middle of back. Using a small, sharp knife, begin at the neck and cut flesh down and away from bones. Remove skeleton, including breastbone; leave thigh and leg intact. Remove and discard wings, if desired. Reserve.

To make the stuffing, combine the cheese, basil, and tomatoes in a bowl. Mix well.

Season the quail inside and out with salt and pepper to taste. Spoon about 2 tablespoons of the cheese mixture onto the middle of the breast of each bird. Bring the sides up to enclose the stuffing and reform the quails to their original shape. Wrap each bird with a slice of bacon or pancetta and secure all quail openings and the bacon ends with toothpicks.

Prepare a covered grill for moderate direct-heat cooking as described on pages 8–10 or according to the manufacturer's instructions. Soak about 2 cups flavorful wood chips.

When the fire is ready, add the presoaked wood chips to the fire. Lightly brush the grill rack with vegetable oil. Brush the quail with melted butter and place on grill rack. Cover the grill and cook, turning and basting frequently with butter, until the skin and bacon are browned and crisp but the meat is still moist inside, about 10 minutes total cooking time.

Nest the quail in radicchio or lettuce leaves, if desired, and garnish with basil sprigs. Serve immediately.

Serves 4.

Apricot-Mustard Glazed Rabbit

My father is a great hunter and my mother often cooked wild rabbit when I was a child. She prepared it quite well I'm sure, but I could never get beyond thinking about Thumper or Bugs. A couple of decades passed before I learned to relish the succulent meat of farm-raised rabbit. This simple method was shown to me by a wholesale purveyor of fancy foods back when I operated Twin Peaks Gourmet in San Francisco and has remained a favorite.

Prepare the glaze and pour into a shallow container.

Quickly rinse the rabbit under cold running water and pat dry with paper toweling. Transfer to the glaze, turning to coat thoroughly. Cover and marinate at room temperature for 2 hours, or in the refrigerator for at least 6 hours or as long as overnight; turn the pieces occasionally. Return to room temperature before cooking.

Prepare a covered grill for moderate indirect-heat cooking as described on pages 8–10 or according to the manufacturer's instructions. Position a drip pan in the center of the fuel grate.

When the fire is ready, lightly brush the grill rack with vegetable oil. Remove the rabbit and reserve the glaze. Place the rabbit on the grill over the drip pan. Cover the grill and cook, basting occasionally with the glaze, until the meat near the bone is no longer pink when tested by cutting with a small, sharp knife at the thickest point, about 30 to 35 minutes.

Arrange a bed of parsley on a platter or 4 dinner plates. Place rabbit on top and garnish with tomatoes. Serve immediately.

Serves 4.

Apricot-Mustard Glaze (page 85)
1 frying rabbit (about 3 pounds),
    cut into serving pieces
Vegetable oil for brushing grill rack
Fresh parsley sprigs, preferably
    flat-leaf type, for garnish
Tiny cherry tomatoes for garnish

SUGGESTED ACCOMPANIMENT
Potato gratin

Honey-Glazed Pork Tenderloin

Here's another recipe from my brother-in-law John Richardson, who serves it alongside my sister's spicy beans. Use a favorite recipe for cooking the beans, but be sure to add plenty of garlic and red pepper. Presoaked wood chips thrown on the fire adds a special smoky flavor to the meat.

Prepare the spice mix; reserve.

Quickly rinse the tenderloins under cold running water and pat dry with paper toweling. Rub the spice mix all over the tenderloins and let stand at room temperature for about 30 minutes.

Prepare a covered grill for moderately low indirect-heat cooking as described on pages 8–10 or according to the manufacturer's instructions. Position a drip pan in the center of the fuel grate. Soak a handful of hickory or other flavorful wood chips.

Prepare the glaze and lightly brush it over the tenderloins.

When the fire is ready, lightly brush the grill rack with vegetable oil. Place the tenderloins on the grill directly over the fire and sear briefly on all sides. Add the presoaked wood chips to the fire, position the meat over the drip pan, and cover the grill. Cook the tenderloins, turning every 10 to 15 minutes and brushing with the glaze, until the internal temperature reads 140° to 145° F on an instant-read thermometer inserted into the thickest part, or until the meat is still pale pink, about 45 minutes to 1 hour. If cooking over wood or charcoal, add more fuel and adjust the air vents as needed to maintain an even temperature.

Transfer the tenderloins to a cutting surface, cover loosely with foil, and let stand about 5 minutes. Cut crosswise into slices about ¼ inch thick. Arrange on preheated plates and serve immediately.

Serves 4 to 6.

Herb-and-Garlic Spice Mix (page 83)
2 pork tenderloins
(about 1 pound *each*), trimmed
of excess fat
Honey-Mustard Glaze (page 85)
Vegetable oil for brushing grill rack

SUGGESTED ACCOMPANIMENTS
Spicy black or red chili beans
Corn bread sticks

Curried Yogurt–Crusted Pork Chops

Curried Yogurt Marinade (page 83)
6 pork loin chops, preferably boned
Salt
Freshly ground black pepper
Vegetable oil for brushing grill rack
Fresh mint sprigs for garnish

SUGGESTED ACCOMPANIMENT
Grilled melon slices or peach halves

Yogurt forms a crust around the chops and keeps the pork from drying out.

Prepare the marinade; reserve.

Quickly rinse the pork chops under cold running water and pat dry with paper toweling. Season to taste with salt and pepper and place in a shallow container. Cover with the marinade and turn chops to coat thoroughly. Cover and refrigerate overnight; turn the pork occasionally. Return to room temperature before cooking.

Prepare a covered grill for moderate direct-heat cooking as described on pages 8–10 or according to the manufacturer's instructions.

When the fire is ready, lightly brush the grill rack with vegetable oil. Remove the pork from the marinade and place on the grill rack to sear 1 minute. Turn and sear second side 1 minute. Cover the grill and cook until the internal temperature registers 140° to 145° when an instant-read thermometer is inserted, or until the meat is pale pink when cut with a small, sharp knife, about 12 to 15 minutes longer.

Arrange on preheated plates, garnish with mint, and serve immediately.

Serves 6.

Maple Baby Back Ribs

Tender meaty pork ribs are always popular grill fare. When unavailable, substitute preseparated, meaty, country-style ribs; allow three or four per person. The smoky flavor gained from adding presoaked hickory, mesquite, or oak chips to the fire is essential for great ribs.

Prepare the marinade; reserve.

Quickly rinse the ribs under cold running water and pat dry with paper toweling. Place in a shallow nonreactive container, pour the marinade over, and turn to coat thoroughly. Cover and refrigerate for at least 12 hours or up to 2 days; turn ribs occasionally. Return to room temperature before cooking.

Preheat an oven to 300° F.

Remove the rib racks and reserve the marinade. Arrange the ribs in an ovenproof pan and bake for about 50 minutes to tenderize.

Prepare a covered grill for moderate direct-heat cooking as described on pages 8–10 or according to the manufacturer's instructions. Soak about 3 cups hickory or other flavorful wood chips in water.

Strain the marinade into a saucepan and cook over high heat until reduced to about 1½ cups.

When the fire is ready, add the presoaked wood chips to the fire and lightly brush the grill rack with vegetable oil. Place the ribs on the rack, cover the grill, and cook, turning and brushing frequently with the reduced marinade, until the meat is tender and well glazed, about 30 minutes.

Transfer to a cutting surface and slice into individual ribs. Serve the ribs piping hot.

Serves 4 to 6.

Maple Marinade (page 84)
4 racks (about 1½ pounds *each*)
   baby back pork ribs,
   cracked along backbone
Vegetable oil for brushing grill rack

SUGGESTED ACCOMPANIMENT
Cole slaw with roasted peanuts

Mixed Sausage Grill

18 assorted sausages (see
recipe introduction)
Vegetable oil for brushing grill rack
Assorted prepared mustards
Fresh herb sprigs such as bay,
rosemary, or sage

SUGGESTED ACCOMPANIMENTS

Crisp green salad
Grilled polenta rounds or
a potato dish

One of my favorite quick ways to entertain a crowd is to offer an assortment of sausages hot off the grill. Purchase the sausages at a good charcuterie or meat market and accompany them with a variety of "gourmet" mustards to appeal to all palates. With the current increase in commercial sausage making, the possibilities are endless. I always include both hot varieties, such as Louisiana links, Cajun andouille, Portuguese linguiça, and spicy Italian links, and mild sausages, such as bratwurst, duck, knockwurst, Thai chicken, and sweet Italian links.

Prepare an open grill for moderate direct-heat cooking as described on pages 8–10 or according to the manufacturer's instructions.

Separate sausage links, if necessary. Prick the skins in several places with a small, sharp knife to allow cooking fat to run off.

When the fire is ready, lightly brush the grill rack with vegetable oil. Place the sausages on the rack and cook, turning frequently, until browned on all sides and the interior tests just past the pink stage but still juicy when cut into with a small, sharp knife, about 10 to 15 minutes, depending upon thickness. Adjust the grill vents to cool down the fire should the dripping fat cause excessive flaming.

Spoon the mustards into small bowls. Arrange the sausages on a platter and garnish with herbs.

Serves 6 to 8.

Lamb Chops with
Red Wine Marinade/Sauce

Whether you choose a still-attached rack or individual chops, lamb marinated in full-bodied red wine such as Merlot or Zinfandel is simply marvelous. The marinade is quickly reduced to a sauce for spooning over the grilled meat.

Prepare the marinade in a large, shallow nonreactive bowl. Add the lamb and turn to coat thoroughly. Cover and marinate at room temperature for 4 hours.

Prepare a covered grill for moderate direct-heat cooking as described on pages 8–10 or according to the manufacturer's instructions.

Remove the lamb and reserve the marinade. Sprinkle with salt and pepper to taste.

When the fire is ready, lightly brush the grill rack with vegetable oil. Place the lamb on the rack and cook, turning once and basting frequently with the reserved marinade, until done to preference, about 8 minutes for medium-rare. Cut the rack into individual chops and keep warm.

Strain the remaining marinade into a small pan and boil over high heat until reduced to a few syrupy spoonfuls.

Arrange the chops on preheated plates, drizzle with sauce, and garnish with rosemary and with grapes, if using. Serve immediately.

Serves 4.

Red Wine Marinade/Sauce (page 82)
1 or 2 racks of lamb (2 to 2½ pounds
    total weight),
    or 8 lamb rib chops
Salt
Freshly ground black pepper
Vegetable oil for brushing grill rack
Fresh rosemary sprigs for garnish
Tiny grapes for garnish (optional)

SUGGESTED ACCOMPANIMENT
Grilled red onions and sweet peppers

Skewered Lamb

Onion Marinade (page 82)
1 leg of lamb (about 5 pounds),
    boned and cut into 1-inch cubes
3 medium-sized leeks, including
    some of the green portion,
    cut into 1-inch pieces, or 2 red
    onions, cut into small wedges
1 red sweet pepper, stem, seeds, and
    membranes discarded, cut into
    1-inch squares
1 pound fresh mushrooms
About 20 cherry tomatoes
Salt
Freshly ground black pepper
Vegetable oil for brushing grill rack
Minced fresh thyme or parsley

SUGGESTED ACCOMPANIMENTS
White rice or couscous
Cucumber salad

Americans have adopted classic Middle Eastern kabobs as their very own.

Prepare the marinade in a large, shallow nonreactive bowl. Add the lamb and turn to coat all sides of the meat. Cover and marinate at room temperature for 3 to 5 hours.

Prepare a covered grill for moderate direct-heat cooking as described on pages 8–10 or according to the manufacturer's instructions. If using bamboo skewers, cover skewers with water and soak for about 20 minutes before threading meat on them.

Remove the lamb and reserve the marinade. Thread the meat on metal or presoaked bamboo skewers. Thread each type of vegetable on separate skewers. Sprinkle meat and vegetables with salt and pepper to taste.

When the fire is ready, lightly brush the grill rack with vegetable oil. Place skewers on the rack, cover the grill, and cook, turning several times and basting meat and vegetables frequently with the reserved marinade, until the lamb is done to preference, about 8 minutes for medium-rare. Remove each vegetable as it is done, about 5 to 10 minutes. Slide the meat and vegetables off the skewers and arrange on preheated plates. Sprinkle with minced thyme or parsley.

Serves 8.

Herb-Crusted Butterflied Leg of Lamb

Among the grandest grilled fare is a succulent leg of lamb boned and spread out in one piece. Most butchers will be glad to do this time-consuming task, if given ample notice.

Herbes de Provence is a highly aromatic blend of dried herbs available in specialty food stores. To prepare the blend at home, combine equal portions of dried whole-leaf marjoram, rosemary, summer savory, and thyme with a sprinkling of dried lavender blossoms and fennel seed.

Prepare the marinade, reducing the amount of olive oil to ¼ cup to create a paste.

Quickly rinse the lamb under cold running water and pat dry with paper toweling. Place in a shallow nonreactive container and rub all over with the marinade paste. Cover and refrigerate overnight; return to room temperature before cooking.

Prepare the chutney; reserve.

Prepare a covered grill for moderate indirect-heat cooking as described on pages 8–10 or according to the manufacturer's instructions. Position a drip pan in the center of the fuel grate.

When the fire is ready, lightly brush the grill rack with vegetable oil. Place the lamb on the grill rack, cover the grill, and cook, turning several times, until done to preference, about 35 to 40 minutes total cooking time for medium-rare. Remove from the grill to a cutting surface that collects drippings, cover loosely with foil, and let stand about 10 minutes. Reheat the chutney.

Thinly slice the lamb and fan slices out on preheated plates. Drizzle with any drippings collected in the grill pan and from the cutting surface. Spoon some of the chutney alongside, garnish with lavender, and serve immediately.

Serves 8.

Herbed Olive Oil Marinade
(page 82), prepared with
herbes de Provence
1 leg of lamb (5 to 6 pounds),
trimmed of excess fat, boned,
and butterflied
Peach Chutney (page 92)
Vegetable oil for brushing grill rack
Pesticide-free lavender blossoms
for garnish

SUGGESTED ACCOMPANIMENTS
**Grilled artichoke hearts,
potato wedges, and figs**

Sage-and-Cheese-Stuffed Veal Chops

In this adaptation of an Italian grilling method, thinly pounded veal with a cheese stuffing is cooked quickly over a medium-hot fire. The cheese stuffing keeps the meat moist and succulent. A bed of soft, fluffy polenta (page 69) is a perfect accompaniment.

Using a small, sharp knife and starting at the meaty side, cut the veal chops horizontally across to the bone. Working with 1 chop at a time, fold one side of the meat back over the bone and place the other side of the butterflied chop between 2 sheets of waxed paper. Beginning at the bone and working toward the edge, pound the meat with a wooden mallet, the flat side of a cleaver, or other flat instrument to a uniform thickness of about ¼ inch, being careful not to make holes in the meat. Repeat with the other half of the chop.

Prepare an open grill for hot direct-heat cooking as described on pages 8–10 or according to the manufacturer's instructions.

Prepare the sauce; reserve.

Spread the chops open and season inside and out with salt and pepper to taste. Place a slice of cheese on one side of each chop; fold back any edges of the cheese that extend beyond the meat. Lay the sage leaves on top of the cheese. Bring the other side of the meat over the stuffing to cover completely. Stitch the 2 pieces of meat together with a needle and cotton string or skewer them together with toothpicks. Brush the chops on both sides with olive oil.

When the fire is ready, lightly brush the grill rack with vegetable oil. Place the chops on the rack and cook, turning several times, just until lightly browned and the cheese has melted, about 7 to 8 minutes total cooking time. Remove thread or toothpicks before serving.

Ladle some of the sauce onto 6 preheated plates and top with a veal chop. Garnish with sage and serve immediately.

Serves 6.

6 rib or loin veal chops,
    about 1½ inches thick
Grilled Tomato and Pepper Sauce
    (page 91)
Salt
Freshly ground black pepper
½ pound fontina or other
    good-melting cheese, cut into
    6 slices each about ¼ inch thick
12 to 18 fresh sage leaves
Fruity olive oil, preferably
    extra-virgin, for brushing veal
Vegetable oil for brushing grill rack
Fresh sage leaves for garnish

SUGGESTED ACCOMPANIMENTS
Polenta
Grilled fennel and sweet pepper

Beef Steak with Wild Mushrooms

Red Wine Marinade/Sauce (page 82)
1 piece (about 2 pounds) top-round
    steak or London broil,
    about 2 inches thick,
    trimmed of excess fat
1 pound fresh wild mushrooms
    such as chanterelles, morels,
    oyster, or shiitake, alone or
    in combination
Vegetable oil for brushing grill rack
Fresh oregano or parsley sprigs,
    preferably flat-leaf type,
    for garnish

SUGGESTED ACCOMPANIMENTS
Grilled tomatoes
Mixed green salad

Juicy beef and mushrooms is a hard-to-beat combination, especially when the mushrooms are flavorful wild varieties that take on a rich mahogany hue on the grill. Fresh domestic mushrooms can be substituted, or presoak about six ounces dried mushrooms.

Prepare the marinade in a large, shallow nonreactive bowl. Add the beef and turn to coat thoroughly. Cover and marinate at room temperature for 3 to 5 hours.

Prepare a covered grill for moderate direct-heat cooking as described on pages 8–10 or according to the manufacturer's instructions. If using bamboo skewers for the mushrooms, cover with water and soak for about 20 minutes before threading mushrooms on them.

Cut large mushrooms into 2 or more pieces; leave small ones whole. Thread the mushrooms on metal or presoaked bamboo skewers.

When the fire is ready, remove the beef and reserve the marinade. Lightly brush the grill rack with vegetable oil. Place the beef on the rack and cook, turning once and brushing with reserved marinade, until done to your preference when cut into with a small, sharp knife, about 15 minutes total cooking time for medium-rare.

About 5 minutes after putting the beef on the grill, place the skewered mushrooms on the grill rack. Cook mushrooms, turning and brushing frequently with some of the marinade, until browned and tender, about 10 minutes. Remove the steak to a cutting surface that collects drippings and let stand about 5 minutes. Remove the mushrooms and keep warm. Strain the marinade into a saucepan and boil over high heat until reduced to a few tablespoons.

Thinly slice the beef on the diagonal and arrange slices slightly overlapping on preheated plates. Drizzle with the reduced marinade and any drippings collected from the cutting surface. Slide the mushrooms off the skewers onto the plates. Garnish with herb sprigs and serve immediately.

Serves 6 to 8.

GRAINS, VEGETABLES, & FRUITS

I'd be hard pressed to choose between hot bread, right off the grill and redolent with fresh garlic and fruity olive oil, and warm slices of creamy polenta crusty from a few minutes over the fire. These simple pleasures represent grilling at its finest.

You'll be missing a treat if you don't throw a few vegetables on the grill alongside the main course. My basic vegetable grilling instructions are followed by a wide variety of seasonal garden delights from which to choose. In addition to serving them as side dishes, grilled vegetables can be tossed with a favorite dressing and served at room temperature as a first course or a salad. Or combine them with cooked pasta, rice, couscous, or another grain and a good vinaigrette or creamy dressing for an unusual hearty salad.

If you've never indulged in fresh fruit warm from a grill, next time place a few pieces on the rack after you take off the main course and serve them for dessert. Update the banana split by starting with a whole banana grilled in its skin until the peel is black; remove the peel and crown the banana with favorite ice creams and a couple of luscious toppings. Or try grilled strawberries over rich vanilla ice cream. For an alternative to apple pie, grill cored apple halves, cut side down, until lightly browned, then turn the apples and mound the cavities with shredded Cheddar or Emmentaler, crumbled creamy blue, or other good-melting cheese and grill until the fruit is tender and the cheese melts.

Grilled fruits also make a grand change-of-pace accompaniment, or an unusual starter to eat while waiting for the main course to come off the grill, especially when offered with a wedge or round of grilled leaf-wrapped cheese.

OTHER GRILLED GRAIN AND VEGETABLE RECIPES IN JAMES McNAIR BOOKS

BAR & GRILL COOKBOOK:

Grilled Escarole, Smoked Ham, and Goat's Cheese, page 54

Grilled Polenta and Sausages with Fresh Tomato Sauce, page 31

Grilled Radicchio, page 26

Grilled Bread with Garlic and Olive Oil

1 or 2 heads garlic
Fruity olive oil, preferably
    extra-virgin
Vegetable oil for brushing grill rack
Italian or French bread,
    preferably whole-grain,
    sliced ¾ to 1 inch thick

A new American grill standard is crusty bread toasted on the grill, rubbed with crushed raw garlic, and generously drizzled with fine olive oil, an idea imported from Italy where it is known as *bruschetta*. In my variation, the hot grilled bread is brushed with olive oil and served with a whole head of grilled garlic. To eat, squeeze a clove of creamy sweet garlic from its charred peel onto the bread and spread with a knife.

Prepare an open grill for moderate direct-heat cooking as described on pages 8–10 or according to the manufacturer's instructions.

Peel away most of the skin from the garlic, leaving the head intact. Brush head all over with olive oil.

When the fire is ready, lightly brush the grill rack with vegetable oil. Place the garlic on the rack and cook, turning several times, until the skin is charred and the inside is soft, about 10 to 20 minutes. Just before serving, add the bread slices and cook, turning once, until toasted to your preference. Brush or drizzle the bread with olive oil and serve with the grilled garlic.

VARIATION: After turning the bread the first time, drizzle the slices with olive oil and move the bread to a cooler part of the grill to keep the bottom from burning. Top each bread slice with a thick slice of Emmentaler, creamy chèvre (goat's milk cheese), fontina, Gruyère, Brie, or other good-melting cheese at room temperature. Grill until the cheese melts.

Herbed Polenta

Make the polenta loaf several hours or a day ahead of grilling slices. To serve soft polenta as a bed under grilled meats, cook the polenta while the meat is on the grill and pour it onto a platter or individual plates. Omit both the herbs and cheese if you prefer plain polenta.

In a deep saucepan, combine the water and the stock or broth, if using, and bring to a boil over high heat. Stir in the salt and reduce the heat to maintain the liquid at a simmer. While stirring continuously with a long-handled wooden spoon, slowly add the polenta in a steady stream. Cook, stirring almost constantly, until the polenta pulls away from the side of the pan, about 15 to 20 minutes. Remove from the heat; stir in the minced herb, butter, and cheese until the cheese melts. Pour into a lightly greased 9- by 5-inch loaf pan, preferably nonstick, pressing the loaf evenly into the corners. Cover with plastic wrap and refrigerate for several hours or up to 3 days.

Prepare an open grill for moderate direct-heat cooking as described on pages 8–10 or according to the manufacturer's instructions.

Briefly dip the bottom half of the polenta pan into hot water, then run a blunt knife around the pan edges to loosen polenta. Invert the polenta onto a flat surface and remove the pan. Cut in slices about ½ inch thick; trim slices into squares or diagonals, or cut into rounds with a cookie cutter, if desired. Brush the slices on both sides with olive oil.

When the fire is ready, lightly brush the grill rack with vegetable oil. Place the polenta on the rack and cook, carefully turning once, until lightly browned and crisp. Sprinkle with Parmesan cheese, garnish with herb sprigs and the tomatoes, if using, and serve immediately.

Serves 6 to 8.

VARIATION: For white polenta, use coarsely ground white cornmeal or grits.

2 cups water, or 6 cups water, if not using stock or broth
4 cups homemade chicken stock or canned chicken broth (optional)
1 tablespoon salt, or to taste
2 cups polenta or coarsely ground yellow cornmeal
2 tablespoons minced fresh rosemary or sage, or 2 teaspoons crumbled dried rosemary or sage
½ cup (1 stick) unsalted butter
⅔ cup freshly grated Parmesan cheese, preferably Parmigiano-Reggiano
Fruity olive oil, preferably extra-virgin, for brushing polenta
Vegetable oil for brushing grill rack
Freshly grated Parmesan cheese, preferably Parmigiano-Reggiano, for sprinkling
Fresh rosemary sprigs or sage leaves for garnish
Halved cherry tomatoes for garnish (optional)

Sesame Tofu

2 packages firm tofu (14 to 18 ounces
    each), sliced into slabs
    about 1 inch thick
Sesame Marinade (page 84)
½ cup sesame seeds, preferably black
8 green onions, including roots and
    some of the green tops,
    cut into 1-inch lengths
Vegetable oil for brushing grill rack

SUGGESTED ACCOMPANIMENTS
White rice
Grilled Asian-type eggplant
Grilled pineapple or papaya

Even nonvegetarians won't miss animal protein when served this intensely flavored soybean curd with a crispy crust.

Drain the tofu and arrange it in a single layer on a baking sheet or tray lined with several thicknesses of paper toweling. Cover with more paper toweling and a second baking sheet or tray and place several heavy objects such as bowls or canned foods on top to weight down the tofu. Let stand for 1 or 2 hours to remove excess moisture.

Prepare the marinade; reserve.

Cut each slab of drained tofu into 4 rectangles and arrange them in a shallow nonreactive container. Pour the marinade over the tofu, cover, and refrigerate for at least 24 hours or as long as 6 days. Return to room temperature before grilling.

An hour or so before cooking, place the sesame seeds in a small, heavy skillet over medium heat and toast, shaking pan or stirring frequently, until white seeds are lightly golden or black seeds are fragrant, about 5 minutes. Pour onto a plate to cool.

Prepare an open grill for moderate direct-heat cooking as described on pages 8–10 or according to the manufacturer's instructions. Cover 8 bamboo skewers with water and soak for about 20 minutes.

Remove the tofu and reserve the marinade. Beginning with the root end, thread the onion pieces lengthwise on presoaked skewers alternately with the tofu. Order the onion pieces to simulate the look of a whole onion.

When the fire is ready, lightly brush the grill rack with vegetable oil. Place the skewered tofu on the rack and cook, turning to grill each side and brushing frequently with the marinade, until lightly browned on all sides, about 12 to 15 minutes.

Sprinkle the tofu with reserved sesame seeds, arrange on preheated plates, and serve immediately.

Serves 4.

Mixed Vegetable Grill

Here's a feast that can serve as a main event or as a starter while meats or fish are grilling. If served as an entrée, plan on about eight ounces of raw vegetables per person. Thread on skewers or place in a hinged wire grill basket, if desired, to make turning easier.

Since vegetables contain little or no fat, brush them with oil or an oil-based marinade to keep them moist and prevent them from sticking to the grill. Such bland vegetable oils as safflower, peanut, or canola (rapeseed) will accomplish these tasks, but a variety of other oils, including a fruity olive oil or a nut oil, will double as flavor enhancers. For a distinctive change of pace, marinate in or brush with hot chili oil or mahogany-hued Asian-style sesame oil.

If you need to reduce fats in your diet, wrap vegetables in banana, cabbage, grape, lettuce, or spinach leaves; wrappers will char without flaming and add a slightly smoky taste to the vegetables.

Prepare the sauce and vegetables; reserve.

Prepare an open grill for moderate to low direct-heat cooking as described on pages 8–10 or according to the manufacturer's instructions.

When the fire is ready, lightly brush the grill rack with vegetable oil. Brush the vegetables with olive oil and season to taste with salt and pepper. Place vegetables on the grill rack over the hottest area of the fire for about 1 minute to sear. Turn and sear on second side 1 minute. Move the vegetables to a cooler area and cook, turning frequently and brushing with oil as necessary, until just tender when pierced with a wooden skewer; see vegetable listings on the following pages for approximate cooking times.

Arrange the vegetables on preheated plates with some of the reserved sauce. Garnish with herbs and serve immediately.

Serves 4.

Garlic Sauce, Spicy Variation
(page 88)
About 4 pounds assorted vegetables
(see pages 74–75 for suggestions)
Vegetable oil for brushing grill rack
Fruity olive oil, preferably
extra-virgin, or other oil
(see recipe introduction)
for brushing vegetables
Salt
Freshly ground black pepper
Fresh herb sprigs such as basil,
flat-leaf parsley, or marjoram
for garnish

FRESH VEGETABLES
FOR GRILLING

COOKED BEFORE GRILLING

The following vegetables should be at least partially cooked before grilling. After precooking, pat them dry with paper toweling, marinate or brush with selected oil, and grill until tender and lightly browned.

ARTICHOKES. Trim off tough lower leaves close to stem. Slice off thorny top third of leaves and shorten stem to about ¾ inch; peel attached stem. As you finish trimming each artichoke, immediately drop it into water to cover to which a little freshly squeezed lemon juice has been added. Steam, boil, or microwave until tender when pierced, about 30 to 50 minutes. Drain and cool. Cut in half lengthwise or into quarters and scoop out and discard the fuzzy chokes. Grill for about 5 to 10 minutes.

ASPARAGUS. Discard tough ends and peel lower portion of stems. Blanch, steam, or microwave stalks for about 3 minutes; grill for about 3 minutes.

BEETS. Steam, boil, or microwave unpeeled beets until just tender, 20 to 50 minutes, depending upon size. Cool and peel. Leave small beets whole or cut in half; slice larger ones. Grill for about 5 to 10 minutes, depending upon size.

No precooking is required for these vegetables. Simply trim as suggested and marinate or brush with selected oil (except corn in husks). Grill over a moderate to low fire as described on the preceding page until just tender and lightly browned.

Corn. To grill in husks, choose ears with ends intact. Pull the husks back but leave attached at base; remove silks. Rub kernels with softened butter, if desired, and reposition husks. Tie narrow end together with a strip of torn husk or cotton string. Soak in water to cover for 15 to 20 minutes. Pat dry with paper toweling and grill for about 15 to 20 minutes.

To grill shucked and silked corn, leave whole or cut into short lengths. Brush with melted butter or vegetable oil and grill for about 5 to 10 minutes.

Eggplant. Leave very small eggplant whole. Cut off stem of larger eggplant and slice lengthwise in half or into wedges, or cut crosswise into thick slices. Leave stems on slender Asian varieties and slice 3 or 4 times lengthwise almost to the stem, then fan out slices on grill rack. Grill for about 15 minutes.

Fennel. Cut bulb into wedges or thick slices. Grill for about 15 minutes.

Garlic. Peel off most of the outer layers of skin and grill for about 20 minutes.

Green onions. Slice off root end and trim off some of the green end. Grill for about 7 to 10 minutes.

Greens. Halve Belgian endive and radicchio. Grill for about 5 minutes.

Leeks. Slice off root end and trim away some of the green tops. Cut in half lengthwise. Or leave whole, but split lengthwise to within a couple inches of the root end and rinse well between layers. Grill for about 5 to 10 minutes.

Mushrooms. Cut off tough portion of stem ends. Leave mushrooms whole or cut very large ones into pieces; skewer if desired. Grill for about 4 to 5 minutes.

Onions. Cut unpeeled onions in half or into quarters and grill for about 15 to 20 minutes. Or thickly slice peeled onions and grill for about 5 minutes.

Peppers. Both sweet peppers and chilies can be grilled whole or cut. To cook whole, grill until skin is charred, transfer to a paper bag, and close to sweat for 15 minutes. Rub off blackened skin with fingertips and remove stems, seeds, and membranes. To cook cut, halve lengthwise and discard stems, seeds, and membranes; cut into wide strips if desired. Grill for about 8 to 10 minutes.

Potatoes, sweet potatoes, and yams. These tubers are all treated in the same way. To grill whole, prick unpeeled potatoes in several places with the tines of a fork and grill until tender, about 25 to 30 minutes for small potatoes and 1 hour or more for large potatoes. Or cut small potatoes in half and larger ones into wedges or ½-inch-thick slices and grill for about 30 minutes. If you wish to shorten grilling time, boil potatoes until almost tender, about 20 to 25 minutes for whole potatoes and about 10 minutes for wedges or slices; grill until browned, about 10 to 15 minutes.

Shallots. Peel and grill for about 3 to 4 minutes.

Summer squash. Leave small squash whole. Slice larger ones in half lengthwise or into quarters, or cut on the diagonal into ½-inch-thick slices. Grill for about 5 to 10 minutes.

Tomatoes. Grill cherry or small tomatoes whole. Cut larger ones in half or into thick slices. Grill for about 8 to 15 minutes.

BROCCOLI. Trim into spears. Blanch, steam, or microwave for about 3 minutes; grill for about 5 minutes.

CARROTS OR PARSNIPS. Steam, boil, or microwave until just tender, about 5 to 12 minutes, depending upon size. Leave small ones whole; thickly slice large ones on the diagonal or cut into quarters. Grill for about 10 minutes.

CAULIFLOWER. Slice into wedges. Blanch or steam for about 6 to 7 minutes; grill for about 7 to 8 minutes.

TURNIPS OR RUTABAGAS. Peel and slice about ½ inch thick. Blanch or steam for about 10 minutes; grill for about 10 to 12 minutes.

WINTER SQUASH. Peel and cut into ½-inch-thick slices. Blanch or steam for about 5 minutes; grill for about 10 to 15 minutes.

Peaches and Cheese

Choose a creamy mild chèvre (goat's milk cheese), a triple-cream cheese such as Saint André, or a small wheel of Brie or Camembert. Nectarines can be used in place of peaches.

Prepare an open grill for moderate to low direct-heat cooking as described on pages 8–10 or according to the manufacturer's instructions.

If using fresh grape leaves, blanch them in boiling water for about 10 seconds, then drain, spread out on a flat surface, and pat dry with paper toweling. If using canned leaves, unroll, rinse under cold running water, spread out, and pat dry. Wrap the leaves around the cheese, overlapping them to prevent melting cheese from leaking out the seams. Tie up the bundle with cotton string to hold the leaves intact.

Cut the peaches in half lengthwise, remove pits, and sprinkle cut sides with sugar.

When the fire is ready, lightly brush the grill rack with vegetable oil. Place the peaches, cut side up, and the leaf-wrapped cheese on the rack. Turn the cheese after about 5 minutes. Turn the peaches after the sugar melts, about 6 to 7 minutes, and grill until soft and nicely marked, about 2 to 3 minutes longer.

Transfer the cheese to a serving platter and pull back the leaves from the cheese. Pull the charred skin off the peaches and discard. Arrange the peaches around the cheese. Garnish platter with flowers, if using. To eat, scoop some of the warm cheese onto the peaches.

Serves 4.

2 or 3 large fresh or canned
　　grape leaves
1 small round cheese
　　(see recipe introduction)
4 large freestone peaches
Brown or granulated sugar
Vegetable oil for brushing grill rack
Pesticide-free flowers such as
　　coreopsis or lobelia for garnish
　　(optional)

Tropical Fruits with Coconut Custard and Chocolate Sauces

Coconut Custard Sauce (page 93)
Chocolate Sauce (page 93)
1 medium-sized ripe pineapple
2 large ripe but firm
    mangoes or papayas
2 slightly underripe firm bananas
Vegetable oil for brushing grill rack
Small pesticide-free tropical blossoms
    such as plumeria, baby
    gardenias, or miniature orchids

Exotic flavors of tropical fruits are intensified with grilling. This alluring composed dessert is a crowning touch to a great meal.

Prepare both the sauces; reserve.

Prepare an open grill for moderate to low direct-heat cooking as described on pages 8–10 or according to the manufacturer's instructions.

Trim off the top and cut away the skin of the pineapple. Cut pineapple in ½-inch-thick slices, then cut slices into wedges; remove and discard cores if tough and set wedges aside. Peel the mangoes and slice off flesh in thick lengthwise slabs from the flat sides of the large pit. Cut each slab of pulp into 2 or 3 slices and reserve the slices. Alternatively, peel, halve, and seed the papayas and cut each half into 4 slices; reserve. Slice the unpeeled bananas on the diagonal into pieces about ½ inch thick; reserve.

When the fire is ready, lightly brush the grill rack with vegetable oil. Place the fruit on the rack and cook, carefully turning once, until tender and lightly browned, about 8 to 10 minutes total cooking time.

Meanwhile, reheat the reserved sauces.

To assemble, spoon a thin layer of coconut sauce onto the bottom of 8 dinner plates. Drop dollops of the chocolate sauce over the top of the coconut sauce, then pull a skewer through the sauces to "paint" a design. Carefully pull off and discard peels from the banana slices and arrange the fruit attractively on the sauce. Garnish with a flower and serve immediately.

Serves 8.

MARINADES, GLAZES, & SAUCES

Mix and match the marinades with the preceding recipes or use them to create your own grill favorites. Remember that marinades containing acids should be assembled and used in nonreactive containers such as glass, ceramic, or heavy-duty plastic. As a general rule, meats and poultry should stand in a marinade about 3 hours at room temperature or 6 to 12 hours in the refrigerator to absorb the flavors fully. Fish should not be marinated longer than 30 minutes at room temperature or 2 or 3 hours in the refrigerator to prevent the acid from pickling their delicate flesh. In spite of what you may read elsewhere, the results of my own extensive tests over the years confirm that marinades do not tenderize meats. This conclusion was recently backed up by findings published in *Cook's Magazine*. Marinades do, however, add wonderful flavors.

In a few cases marinades are also reduced over heat to form simple sauces for drizzling over the finished dish.

As with the marinades, the sauces that follow can be combined with a wide variety of grilled fare, allowing you to originate dishes that appeal to your palate.

MARINADES AND SAUCES FOR GRILLED FARE IN OTHER JAMES McNAIR BOOKS

CHICKEN:
Cumberland Marinade, page 78
Korean Barbecue Sauce, page 80
Orange Marinade, page 80
Peanut Sauce, page 82
Provençal Marinade, page 80
Raspberry Marinade, page 78
Sate Marinade, page 82
Tomato Barbecue Sauce, page 84
Yakitori Marinade, page 82

Herbed Olive Oil Marinade

This simple blend imparts subtle flavor to fish or chicken breasts.

1 cup fruity olive oil,
    preferably extra-virgin
2 tablespoons freshly squeezed
    lemon juice or
    white wine vinegar
¼ cup minced fresh herbs such as
    flat-leaf parsley, oregano,
    thyme, or rosemary, alone or
    in combination
2 teaspoons minced or pressed
    garlic
Salt
Freshly ground black pepper
Ground cayenne pepper (optional)

In a nonreactive bowl, combine all ingredients, including salt and peppers to taste. Blend well.

Makes about 1¼ cups.

Red Wine Marinade/Sauce

I prefer making this marinade with Merlot or Zinfandel for lamb and Cabernet Sauvignon or Pinot Noir for beef, venison, or duck.

After marinating and basting the meat, strain the remaining marinade into a saucepan and boil over high heat until reduced to a syrupy sauce. Spoon the sauce over the grilled meat.

1 cup full-bodied dry red wine
1 cup fruity olive oil, preferably
    extra-virgin
3 garlic cloves, minced or pressed
1 bay leaf, crumbled
1 tablespoon minced fresh
    oregano, or 1 teaspoon
    crumbled dried oregano
Salt
Freshly ground black pepper

In a nonreactive bowl, combine all ingredients, including salt and pepper to taste. Blend well.

Makes about 2 cups.

Onion Marinade

Traditional with lamb, but also imparts delicious flavor to beef.

¾ cup fruity olive oil, preferably
    extra-virgin
1½ tablespoons minced fresh
    thyme, or 1½ teaspoons
    crumbled dried thyme
4 bay leaves, crumbled
3 cups grated yellow onion
1 tablespoon minced or pressed
    garlic
½ cup freshly squeezed lemon juice
Salt
Freshly ground black pepper
Tabasco sauce or other
    liquid hot-pepper sauce

In a nonreactive bowl, combine all ingredients, including salt, pepper, and pepper sauce to taste.

Makes about 4¼ cups.

Herb-and-Garlic Spice Mix

Rub this concoction over the surface of meat or fish and let stand at room temperature for about half an hour before grilling.

2 tablespoons minced fresh parsley
2 tablespoons minced fresh oregano, or 2 teaspoons crumbled dried oregano
1½ teaspoons minced fresh rosemary, or ½ teaspoon crumbled dried rosemary
1½ teaspoons minced fresh thyme, or ½ teaspoon crumbled dried thyme
1 tablespoon minced or pressed garlic
1 tablespoon dried beef bouillon base (optional)
1½ teaspoons salt, or to taste
1½ teaspoons freshly ground black pepper, or to taste
1 teaspoon ground cayenne pepper, or to taste

In a small bowl, combine all ingredients; blend well.

Makes about ½ cup.

Curried Yogurt Marinade

In addition to imparting flavor, this blend forms a great crust during grilling that helps keep meat from drying out.

2 cups plain low-fat or nonfat yogurt
2 tablespoons minced or pressed garlic
2 tablespoons chopped fresh ginger root
2 tablespoons olive oil
¼ cup mild or hot curry powder, or to taste
Salt
Freshly ground black pepper

In a food processor or blender, combine yogurt, garlic, ginger, and olive oil; purée until smooth. Blend in curry powder, salt, and pepper to taste.

Makes about 2 cups.

Chili-Coconut Marinade

Spicy, sweet, and with a touch of the exotic.

2 fresh red hot chili peppers, seeded
3 tablespoons chopped shallot or yellow onion
3 tablespoons minced fresh cilantro (coriander), including stems
2 tablespoons minced fresh or thawed frozen galangal root or fresh ginger root
1 tablespoon chopped garlic
1 teaspoon chopped fresh or dried lemongrass or lemon zest
½ cup fish sauce or light soy sauce
½ cup unsweetened coconut milk (see page 93)
3 tablespoons vegetable oil
1 tablespoon granulated sugar

In a food processor or blender, combine chili peppers, shallot or onion, cilantro, galangal or ginger, garlic, and lemongrass or lemon zest; chop finely. Add the fish or soy sauce, coconut milk, oil, and sugar and blend until fairly smooth.

Makes about 2 cups.

Chili Marinade

Great with chicken, turkey, pork, or beef.

1 tablespoon chili powder, preferably from *ancho* or *pasilla* peppers
1 tablespoon minced shallot or red onion
2 teaspoons minced or pressed garlic
¼ cup chopped fresh cilantro (coriander)
2 tablespoons chopped fresh oregano, or 2 teaspoons crumbled dried oregano
1 teaspoon ground cumin
¼ cup freshly squeezed lime or lemon juice
¼ cup fruity olive oil, preferably extra-virgin
Salt
Freshly ground black pepper
Ground cayenne pepper

In a small nonreactive bowl, combine all ingredients; blend well.

Makes about ¾ cup.

Sesame Marinade

Turns bland tofu into a sensational dish, but is also wonderful with meats.

½ cup soy sauce
½ cup red wine
½ cup rice vinegar
½ cup Asian-style sesame oil
¼ cup fruity olive oil, preferably extra-virgin
2 tablespoons hot chili oil, or to taste
1 tablespoon minced or pressed garlic
Salt

In a nonreactive bowl, combine all ingredients; blend well.

Makes about 2¼ cups.

Pineapple Teriyaki Marinade

Try this tropics-inspired marinade on pork, chicken, or firm ocean fish.

1 cup chopped fresh or crushed canned pineapple
¼ cup soy sauce
¼ cup mirin (sweetened rice wine) or dry sherry
1 tablespoon grated fresh ginger root

In a nonreactive bowl, combine all ingredients; blend well.

Makes about 1½ cups.

Maple Marinade

A tasty alternative to the usual tomato-based sauce for pork ribs. Use first as a marinade, then strain and reduce over high heat to form a glaze that can be brushed on meat during grilling.

1½ cups pure maple syrup
1½ cups apple cider vinegar
1 cup peanut, safflower, or other high-quality vegetable oil
½ cup molasses
½ cup light soy sauce
3 tablespoons prepared mustard, preferably California-style sweet type
2 tablespoons juniper berries, crushed

In a nonreactive bowl, combine all ingredients; blend well.

Makes about 5 cups.

Wine and Orange Marinade

This wine-based marinade complements duck, pork, or rabbit.

¼ cup (½ stick) unsalted butter
1 cup freshly squeezed orange juice
½ cup port or red varietal wine
¼ cup honey or firmly packed
    brown sugar
2 tablespoons balsamic or
    red wine vinegar
2 tablespoons soy sauce
1 tablespoon Dijon-style mustard
2 tablespoons minced fresh
    rosemary, or 2 teaspoons
    crumbled dried rosemary
2 teaspoons minced or pressed
    garlic
2 teaspoons minced fresh
    ginger root
Salt
Freshly ground black pepper

Melt the butter in a saucepan over low heat. Add the remaining ingredients, including salt and pepper to taste, and simmer until heated through and flavors are blended, about 5 minutes.

Makes about 2 cups.

Red Wine Jelly

Wine-infused jelly is a sensational glaze for brushing on poultry or pork during grilling. Use port or any hearty, red varietal wine such as Cabernet Sauvignon, Petite Sirah, Merlot, or Zinfandel.

¾ cup water
¼ cup freshly squeezed lemon juice
2 pouches (3 ounces *each*)
    liquid pectin
3 cups red wine (see
    recipe introduction)
4½ cups granulated sugar

In a saucepan over medium-high heat, combine the water, lemon juice, and pectin. Bring to a boil and cook 1 minute. Reduce heat to low, add the wine and sugar, and stir just until the sugar dissolves; to prevent alcohol from evaporating, do not allow to approach a simmer. Pour into containers and seal.

To use as a glaze or sauce, reheat in a saucepan over low heat until melted.

Makes about 4 pints.

Apricot-Mustard Glaze

Compatible with rabbit, chicken, or pork. Brush on meat during grilling, then serve any extra as a sauce.

1 cup apricot preserves
½ cup Dijon-style mustard
¼ cup honey
¼ cup firmly packed brown sugar
¼ cup apple cider vinegar

Combine all ingredients in a saucepan over low heat. Stir to mix, then heat gently until the preserves and sugar melt.

Makes about 2 cups.

Honey-Mustard Glaze

A simple glaze that's great brushed on pork or poultry during grilling.

2 tablespoons coarse-grained
    Dijon-style mustard
2 tablespoons firmly packed
    brown sugar
5 tablespoons honey

Combine all ingredients in a small saucepan and simmer over low heat until the sugar melts, about 5 minutes.

Makes about ½ cup.

Composed Butters

Butter enhanced with fresh herbs makes a simple and delicious sauce for most grilled foods, especially fish. For a whimsical touch, slice the cold butter, trim it with tiny aspic cutters, and place the cutouts on the grilled food just before serving.

To serve the flavored butter as a hot sauce, melt it in a small saucepan and pour over the grilled fare or into a small bowl for dipping.

1 cup (2 sticks) unsalted butter, softened
¼ cup minced fresh herb of choice such as basil, chervil, chives, cilantro (coriander), dill, or tarragon
Freshly squeezed lemon or lime juice
Grated lemon or lime zest
Salt
Freshly ground black or white pepper

Beat the butter in a bowl with a wooden spoon or in an electric mixer, food processor, or blender until light and fluffy. Add the herb and the citrus juice and zest, salt, and pepper to taste; mix well.

Cover and chill for at least 1 hour before serving, or refrigerate for up to 5 days. Or wrap tightly and freeze for up to 3 months. Return almost to room temperature before serving.

Makes about 1 cup.

VARIATIONS: Omit herb and citrus juice and zest. Flavor butter with minced fresh ginger root and a bit of Dijon-style mustard; chopped capers and anchovy fillets; chopped pitted Niçoise olives; or a little wasabi (Japanese horseradish powder).

White Butter (*Beurre Blanc*) or Red Butter (*Beurre Rouge*)

When made with white wine and vinegar, this classic butter sauce is one of the best complements to grilled fish. The red variation is wonderful poured over sliced grilled steak.

⅓ cup minced shallots
⅓ cup dry white or red wine
¼ cup freshly squeezed lemon juice or white or red wine vinegar
1 cup (2 sticks) unsalted butter, cut into 8 equal pieces
Salt
Freshly ground black or white pepper

In a nonreactive saucepan over medium-high heat, combine the shallots, wine, and lemon juice or vinegar. Cook, uncovered, until the shallots are tender but not too dark and the liquid has almost evaporated, about 6 minutes; avoid scorching the shallots.

Remove the pan from the heat and add 1 piece of the butter, stirring with a wooden spoon or wire whisk until the butter melts. Place the pan over low heat and add the remaining butter, 1 piece at a time, stirring after each addition until the butter melts. When all the butter has been added, season to taste with salt and pepper. Serve immediately or place in a double boiler over barely simmering water for up to 30 minutes.

Makes about 1¼ cups.

Toasted Pecan Butter

Sublime topping for grilled fish or chicken.

1½ cups shelled pecans
6 tablespoons (¾ stick) unsalted
    butter, softened
2 tablespoons freshly squeezed
    lemon juice
2 teaspoons Worcestershire sauce

Preheat an oven to 350° F.

Spread the pecans in an ovenproof skillet or on a baking sheet and toast in the oven, stirring occasionally, until lightly browned and fragrant, about 10 minutes. Transfer to a plate to cool.

Place ¾ cup of the nuts in a food processor or blender. Add the butter, lemon juice, and Worcestershire sauce and blend until the consistency of a smooth butter. Reserve at room temperature.

Chop the remaining pecans to use as a garnish over the butter.

Makes about 1 cup.

Champagne Cream

A luxurious topping for grilled oysters, scallops, or other seafood.

1 bottle (750 ml) brut Champagne
    or other sparkling wine
¾ cup minced shallots, or
    1 cup minced yellow onion
2 cups homemade fish stock or
    bottled clam juice
1 quart heavy (whipping) cream
2 tablespoons Worcestershire sauce
½ cup (1 stick) unsalted butter,
    cut into 8 equal pieces
⅓ cup minced fresh chervil
    or other mild herb
Freshly squeezed lemon juice
Salt
Ground cayenne pepper

In a small saucepan over medium-high heat, combine the Champagne or other sparkling wine and shallots. Boil, uncovered, until the liquid is reduced to about ¼ cup, about 20 minutes. Add the fish stock or clam juice and continue boiling until slightly reduced, about 10 minutes. Add the cream and Worcestershire sauce and continue boiling until reduced to about 2 cups, about 20 minutes.

Reduce the heat to low and add the butter, 1 piece at a time, stirring after each addition with a wooden spoon or wire whisk until the butter melts. When all the butter has been added, stir in the chervil and lemon juice, salt, and cayenne pepper to taste.

Makes about 2½ cups.

VARIATION: To make a sauce for grilled poultry, substitute chicken stock for the fish stock or clam juice and use tarragon or basil in place of the chervil.

Creole Mustard Cream

When zesty Creole-style mustard is not available, use a Dijon type or one of the countless gourmet mustards found in specialty markets.

3 tablespoons unsalted butter
1 cup finely chopped sweet red or
    yellow onion
¾ cup dry vermouth or white wine
1½ cups heavy (whipping) cream
½ cup Creole mustard (available
    in specialty food stores and
    some supermarkets)
Salt
Freshly ground black pepper

Melt the butter in a saucepan over low heat. Add the onion and cook, stirring frequently, until soft but not brown, about 4 minutes. Add the vermouth or wine and increase the heat to medium. Cook, uncovered, until the liquid evaporates, about 5 minutes. Stir in the cream and cook until reduced by about one-fourth, about 5 minutes.

Remove pan from the heat and stir in the mustard and salt and pepper to taste. Serve immediately or cover and let stand up to 2 hours. To reheat, place over low heat and stir constantly until warm.

Makes about 1½ cups.

Garlic Sauce *(Aïoli)*

Classic Provençal garlic mayonnaise has become an American favorite with grilled vegetables or fish.

When time is short, blend minced or pressed garlic, mustard, lemon juice, and seasonings to taste into a cup of high-quality commercial mayonnaise.

4 garlic cloves, peeled
1 egg yolk, at room temperature
1 teaspoon Dijon-style mustard
1 tablespoon freshly squeezed
    lemon juice
1 cup fruity olive oil, preferably
    extra-virgin
Salt
Freshly ground white pepper

In a blender or food processor, mince the garlic. Add the egg yolk, mustard, and lemon juice and blend for about 30 seconds. With the motor running at high speed, slowly drizzle in the olive oil in a steady stream and blend until a thick mayonnaise consistency forms. Turn the motor off.

With a rubber or plastic spatula, scrape down oil from sides of container and blend into the sauce. Season to taste with salt and pepper. Use immediately or transfer to a covered container and refrigerate for up to 2 days.

Makes about 1 cup.

SPICY VARIATION: For a zesty version, stir ¾ cup minced red sweet pepper, 2 tablespoons minced sweet pickle, and ¼ teaspoon Tabasco sauce or other liquid hot-pepper sauce, or to taste, into the finished sauce.

Red Hot Chili Mayonnaise

Spoon this spicy mixture onto grilled chicken, pork, or fish.

1 egg, at room temperature
2 egg yolks, at room temperature
1 tablespoon Dijon-style mustard
2 tablespoons freshly squeezed
    lemon juice
½ cup chopped roasted red sweet
    pepper (pages 73–75) or
    canned pimento
1 teaspoon minced *chipotle*
    chili peppers (smoked,
    ripened jalapeños), or to taste
2 cups safflower or other
    high-quality vegetable oil
Salt

In a blender or food processor, combine the egg, egg yolks, mustard, lemon juice, roasted pepper or pimiento, and chili pepper; blend for about 30 seconds. With the motor running at high speed, slowly drizzle in the oil in a steady stream and blend until a thick mayonnaise consistency forms. Turn the motor off.

With a rubber or plastic spatula, scrape down oil from sides of container and blend into the sauce. Add salt to taste. Use immediately or transfer to a covered container and refrigerate for up to 2 days.

Makes about 3 cups.

Remoulade Sauce

This cold concoction is great with grilled fish.

2 cups homemade or high-quality
    commercial mayonnaise
1 tablespoon Dijon-style mustard
1 teaspoon minced or pressed
    garlic
2 tablespoons minced gherkins
2 tablespoons drained capers,
    coarsely chopped
¼ cup minced fresh parsley
2 tablespoons minced fresh herbs
    such as chervil, chives, or
    tarragon, alone or a
    combination
3 anchovy fillets, minced, or
    1 teaspoon anchovy paste
Salt
Freshly ground black pepper

In a bowl, combine all ingredients, including salt and pepper to taste, and mix thoroughly. Transfer to a covered container and refrigerate for at least 2 hours before serving, or store for as long as 4 days.

Makes about 2½ cups.

Summer Garden Salsa

This light and crisp counterpoint to grilled fish, chicken, pork, or veal goes together quickly.

1½ cups finely chopped
    yellow summer squash
1 cup peeled, seeded, and
    finely chopped ripe tomato
½ cup finely chopped green onion,
    including some of the
    green portion
1 teaspoon minced fresh hot chili
    pepper, or to taste
½ teaspoon minced or pressed
    garlic
2 tablespoons minced fresh herbs
    such as basil, marjoram,
    savory, or oregano, alone or
    a combination
Salt
Freshly ground black pepper
¼ cup safflower or other
    high-quality vegetable oil
1½ tablespoons freshly squeezed
    lemon juice

Combine all ingredients in a bowl and mix well. Let stand for about 15 minutes before serving.

Makes about 3¼ cups.

Grilled Vegetable Salsa

This Mediterranean-influenced warm salsa goes with just about any grilled fish, meat, or poultry.

8 fresh baby artichokes
    (about 1 ounce *each*),
    trimmed, or 1 cup drained
    canned artichoke hearts
4 medium-sized tomatoes
1 red or golden sweet pepper
1 medium-sized red or yellow
    onion
About 25 Niçoise or Kalamata
    olives, pitted and quartered
¼ cup drained capers
¼ cup fruity olive oil, preferably
    extra-virgin
2 tablespoons freshly squeezed
    lemon juice
1 cup chopped fresh basil
½ cup finely chopped fresh
    parsley, preferably
    flat-leaf type
Salt
Freshly ground black pepper
Ground cayenne pepper

Grill the artichoke hearts, tomatoes, sweet pepper, and onion as directed on pages 73–75. Remove vegetables to a work surface and let cool until they can be handled. Slice the artichoke hearts. Peel, seed, and chop the sweet pepper and tomatoes and peel and chop the onion.

Combine the grilled vegetables with the olives, capers, oil, lemon juice, basil, parsley, and salt and ground peppers to taste. Serve warm or at room temperature.

Makes about 3 cups.

Pineapple Salsa

This spicy, sweet combination is excellent with fish or chicken.

1 small- to medium-sized
    pineapple, peeled and cored
¾ cup minced red onion
1 cup chopped fresh cilantro
    (coriander)
1 tablespoon rice vinegar or
    white wine vinegar
½ teaspoon ground cayenne
    pepper, or to taste
Salt

Coarsely chop the pineapple and transfer to a colander set over a bowl to drain for about 5 minutes.

Transfer the pineapple to a bowl. Add the onion, cilantro, vinegar, cayenne, and a light sprinkling of salt to taste. Stir to combine, cover, and chill for about 1 hour or as long as several hours.

Makes about 4 cups.

Citrus Salsa

A tangy and sweet foil to spicy grilled dishes.

1 large grapefruit, preferably pink
2 large oranges or tangerines
½ cup minced fresh mint
3 tablespoons minced fresh chives
2 tablespoons freshly squeezed
    lemon or lime juice
1 teaspoon sugar
¼ teaspoon Tabasco sauce or
    other liquid hot-pepper
    sauce, or to taste
Salt

Peel the grapefruit and oranges or tangerines. Section the fruits and remove all white pith and membrane. Coarsely chop the fruits and place in a colander set over a bowl to drain for about 5 minutes.

Transfer the drained fruits to a bowl. Add remaining ingredients, including salt to taste. Stir to combine, cover, and chill for about 1 hour or as long as several hours.

Makes about 3 cups.

Spicy Sweet-and-Sour Dipping Sauce

Immerse bites of hot grilled chicken or other meats into individual bowls of this zippy mixture.

½ cup rice vinegar
½ cup light soy sauce
2 teaspoons granulated sugar
3 tablespoons minced or pressed
   garlic
1 tablespoon minced fresh
   red hot chili pepper
¼ cup Asian-style sesame oil
1 tablespoon hot chili oil,
   or to taste
1 tablespoon minced fresh
   cilantro (coriander)

In a saucepan over medium-high heat, combine the vinegar, soy sauce, sugar, garlic, and chili pepper. Cook, stirring, just until the sugar melts.

Transfer to a bowl and immediately blend in the oils. Cool, then stir in the cilantro.

Makes about 1½ cups.

Grilled Tomato and Pepper Sauce

Try this smoky twist on tomato sauce. Combine red tomatoes and peppers or use golden varieties.

3 pounds flavorful ripe tomatoes
2 large sweet peppers
1 teaspoon minced or pressed
   garlic
3 bay leaves
3 tablespoons minced fresh thyme,
   or 1 tablespoon crumbled
   dried thyme
¾ cup homemade chicken stock or
   canned chicken broth
2 tablespoons balsamic or red wine
   vinegar
½ cup heavy (whipping) cream
½ cup (1 stick) unsalted butter
Salt
Ground cayenne pepper

Grill tomatoes and sweet peppers as directed on pages 73–75. Remove to a work surface to cool, then peel, seed, and chop. Transfer pulp and any collected juices to a saucepan. Add garlic, bay leaves, and thyme and cook over medium heat until liquid evaporates, about 20 minutes. Discard bay leaves and place tomato-pepper mixture in a food processor or blender. Purée until smooth.

Return the puréed mixture to the saucepan, stir in the stock or broth and vinegar, and cook over medium-low heat until thick. Stir in the cream and butter. Season to taste with salt and cayenne pepper.

Makes about 3 cups.

Gingered Mango Sauce

Also good with grilled pork, this luxurious sauce transforms grilled fish or scallops into a tropical treat.

2 tablespoons unsalted butter
6 tablespoons chopped shallots or
    yellow onion
2 tablespoons minced fresh
    ginger root
1 teaspoon minced or pressed
    garlic
1 cup dry white wine
2 ripe mangoes, peeled and pitted
1 cup homemade fish or chicken
    stock or canned chicken
    broth
½ cup heavy (whipping) cream,
    light cream, or half-and-half
¼ cup freshly squeezed lime juice
Salt
Freshly ground white pepper
¼ cup chopped fresh mint

Melt the butter in a saucepan over medium-high heat. Add the shallots or onion and ginger and sauté until soft but not brown, about 5 minutes. Add the garlic and sauté 1 minute longer. Pour in the wine and cook until the wine is reduced to about ¼ cup.

Transfer the mixture to a food processor or blender. Add the mango pulp and fish or chicken stock or chicken broth and purée until smooth. Return the mixture to the saucepan over medium-high heat. Add the cream, lime juice, and salt and pepper to taste; cook until the sauce is reduced by half. Stir in the mint just before serving.

Makes about 2 cups.

Peach or Rhubarb Chutney

A quick sweet-tart condiment that goes well with duck or other poultry, as well as with grilled pork.

1½ pounds peeled, pitted,
    and chopped peaches, or
    1½ pounds rhubarb, peeled if
    tough, and sliced about
    ½ inch thick
6 tablespoons apple cider vinegar
2 tablespoons freshly squeezed
    lemon juice
½ cup raisins
¼ cup minced white onion
2 tablespoons slivered preserved
    ginger
1½ teaspoons salt, or to taste
½ teaspoon ground allspice
¼ teaspoon ground cloves
¼ teaspoon ground ginger
2 cups granulated sugar,
    or to taste
¼ cup port

Combine all ingredients in a large saucepan and cook over medium heat until thick, about 30 minutes. Serve warm or cover and refrigerate for up to 1 week; reheat before serving.

Makes 3 to 4 cups.

Coconut Custard Sauce

Included here to finish off Grilled Tropical Fruits (page 79), this sauce is also delicious over plain cakes or fruit pies.

If you cannot locate canned coconut milk, combine 2 cups heated light cream or half-and-half with the grated meat from a fresh coconut or 4 cups grated unsweetened dried coconut and then let stand for 30 minutes. Strain the liquid through cheesecloth, squeezing cloth to extract all the milk.

1 cup granulated sugar
1 cup water
2 cups canned coconut milk
    (available in specialty food
    shops and some
    supermarkets)
6 egg yolks, at room temperature,
    well beaten
2 tablespoons light rum, or
    1 teaspoon vanilla extract

In a saucepan over high heat, combine the sugar and water. Cook, stirring, until the sugar dissolves. Continue cooking without stirring until the syrup reaches 230° F (soft-ball stage) on a candy thermometer. Remove from the heat and whisk in the coconut milk.

Pour about ½ cup of the mixture into the egg yolks and beat until smooth. Slowly whisk the egg yolk mixture into the saucepan. Place over low heat and cook, stirring constantly, until thickened, about 5 minutes. Remove from the heat, cool slightly, then stir in rum or vanilla.

To reheat, stir over low heat.

Makes about 2 cups.

Chocolate Sauce

If made ahead, cool, then cover and refrigerate. To reheat, stir over low heat.

8 ounces semisweet chocolate,
    chopped
2 tablespoons unsalted butter
1 cup heavy (whipping) cream
1 teaspoon vanilla extract

In a saucepan over low heat, combine the chocolate, butter, and cream. Cook, stirring frequently, until the chocolate is melted and the mixture is smooth. Alternatively, melt and blend the mixture in the microwave on medium power, stirring frequently.

Remove from the heat and stir in the vanilla extract. Serve immediately or cover and refrigerate.

Makes about 2 cups.

Index

Barbecuing defined 5
Basting brushes 6
Briquettes 5, 8

Charcoal 5, 6, 8
Charcoal grills 6
Cleaning brush 6
Covered grills 7

Direct-heat grilling 9
Drip pans 6

Electric grills 7
Extinguishing fires 11

Fire starter 6, 8-9
Fuels 6-7, 8

Gas 6-7, 8
Gas grills 6-7
Grilling defined 5
Grilling tips 10-11
Grill types 6-7

Health 11
Hinged wire grills 6-7, 10
Hot fire defined 10

Indirect grilling 9

Lump charcoal 8

Mitts 7
Moderate fire defined 10

Open versus closed 7

Safety 10
Skewers 7
Smoke 9
Spatula 7
Starting fires 8-9

Thermometer 7
Tongs 7
Tools 6-7

Wood chips 9

Recipe Index

Aïoli 88
Apricot-Mustard Glaze 85
Apricot-Mustard Glazed Rabbit 45

Beef Steak with Wild Mushrooms 62
Beurre Blanc 86
Beurre Rouge 86
Bread, Grilled 66
Butters, Composed 86

Catfish, Spicy 25
Chapagne Cream 87
Cheese, Peaches and 77
Chicken, Pineapple 37
Chicken, Spicy Young 34
Chili-Coconut Marinade 83
Chili Marinade 84
Chili-Marinated Turkey with
    Pineapple Salsa 39
Chocolate Sauce 93
Citrus Salsa 90
Coconut Custard Sauce 93
Composed Butters 86
Creole Mustard Cream 88
Curried Yogurt-Crusted
    Pork Chops 48
Curried Yogurt Marinade 83

Duck Breast with Red Wine Jelly 41

Fish, Skewered 30
Fish Steak with Gingered
    Mango Sauce 22
Fish, Whole 26
Fruits, Tropical 78

Garlic Sauce *(Aïoli)* 88
Gingered Mango Sauce 92
Gorgonzola-Stuffed Quail 42
Grilled Bread with Garlic and
    Olive Oil 66
Grilled Tomato and Pepper Sauce 91
Grilled Vegetable Salsa 90

Herb-and-Garlic Spice Mix 83
Herb-Crusted Butterflied
    Leg of Lamb 59
Herb-Marinated Shrimp 14
Herbed Olive Oil Marinade 82
Herbed Polenta 69
Honey-Glazed Pork Tenderloin 47
Honey-Mustard Glaze 85

Lamb, Herb-Crusted Butterflied
    Leg of 59
Lamb Chops with Red Wine
    Marinade/Sauce 55
Lamb, Skewered 56
Lobster with Lemon-Chive Butter 20

Maple Baby Back Ribs 51
Maple Marinade 84
Mayonnaise, Red Hot Chili 89
Mixed Sausage Grill 52
Mixed Vegetable Grill 73-75

Onion Marinade 82
Oysters with Champagne Cream 17

Peach or Rhubarb Chutney 92
Peaches and Cheese 77
Pineapple Chicken 37
Pineapple Salsa 90
Pineapple Teriyaki Marinade 84
Polenta, Herbed 69
Pork Chops, Curried
    Yogurt-Crusted 48
Pork Tenderloin, Honey-Glazed 47

Quail, Gorgonzola-Stuffed 42

Rabbit, Apricot-Mustard Glazed 45
Remoulade Sauce 89
Red Butter *(Beurre Rouge)* 86
Red Hot Chili Mayonnaise 89
Red Wine Jelly 85
Red Wine Marinade/Sauce 82
Ribs, Maple Baby Back 51

Sage-and-Cheese-Stuffed
    Veal Chops 61
Salsas 89-90
Sausage, Mixed Grill 52
Scallops with Squid-Ink Pasta 18
Sesame Marinade 84
Sesame Tofu 70
Shrimp, Herb-Marinated 14
Skewered Fish 30
Skewered Lamb 56
Spicy Catfish Fillets with
    Remoulade Sauce 25

Spicy Sweet-and-Sour
    Dipping Sauce 91
Spicy Young Chicken 34
Steak, Beef 62
Summer Garden Salsa 89

Toasted Pecan Butter 87
Tofu, Sesame 70
Tropical Fruits with Coconut
    Custard and Chocolate Sauces 78
Trout with Toasted Pecan Butter 28
Turkey, Chili-Marinated 39

Veal Chops,
    Sage-and-Cheese-Stuffed 61
Vegetable, Mixed Grill 73-75

White Butter *(Beurre Blanc)* 86
Whole Fish with Grilled
    Vegetable Salsa 26
Wine and Orange Marinade 85

ACKNOWLEDGMENTS

All china, crystal, and silver have been graciously provided by Tiffany and Company, San Francisco.

Special thanks to Michael Barcun for making the contact with Tiffany and to Bill Peabody and Michael Mosser for their invaluable assistance in selecting appropriate patterns.

To Toshiko Chang at Britex Fabrics for her keen eye in assisting with choosing fabrics for the table linens.

To Jack Jensen at Chronicle Books for suggesting this book, and to the entire staff for all their efforts toward making my series successful.

To wordsmith Sharon Silva for another superb round of copy editing.

To friends and family who shared recipes, ideas, and encouragement and looked after my house and garden while I was in hibernation writing, especially D. Arvid Adams, John Carr, Louis Hicks, Gail and Tad High, Douglas Jackson, Mark Leno, Alan May, Marian May, Martha McNair, Devereux McNair, John Richardson, Kristi and Bob Spence, and Chuck Swanson.

To Rosie (aka Sue Dunsford) of the Calistoga Inn for sharing her award-winning duck ideas.

To Patricia Brabant for another sterling achievement in photography, and for her talent for making the whole process fun. And to her very able assistant M. J. Murphy for her countless contributions and refreshing humor.

To Cleve Gallat and Charles Sublett of CTA Graphics for another excellent job of turning my manuscript and layouts into finished pages.

To my assistant Ellen Quan for the many contributions she made while simultaneously finishing her final semester toward a degree in hotel and restaurant management.

To my loyal companions Addie Prey, Buster Booroo, Michael T. Wigglebutt, Joshua J. Chew, and Dweasel Pickle, who hung around the grill anxiously awaiting the tasty results as recipes were developed.

To Lin Cotton, my partner, who adds creative fuel to all my work.